Reconceptualizing Leadership in the Early Years

Reconceptualizing Leadership in the Early Years

Rory McDowall Clark and Janet Murray

Open University Press

Open University Press
McGraw-Hill Education
McGraw-Hill House
Shoppenhangers Road
Maidenhead
Berkshire
England
SL6 2QL

email: enquiries@openup.co.uk
world wide web: www.openup.co.uk

and Two Penn Plaza, New York, NY 10121-2289, USA

First published 2012

A catalogue record of this book is available from the British Library

ISBN-13: 9780335246243 (pb)
ISBN-10: 0335246249 (pb)
eISBN: 9780335246250

Library of Congress Cataloging-in-Publication Data
CIP data applied for

Typesetting and e-book compilations by
RefineCatch Limited, Bungay, Suffolk
Printed in the UK by Bell & Bain Ltd, Glasgow

Fictitious names of companies, products, people, characters and/or data that may be used herein (in case studies or in examples) are not intended to represent any real individual, company, product or event.

The *McGraw·Hill* Companies

"This book makes an innovative contribution to the discussion and debate about leadership in early years. The new conceptual framework which is introduced for understanding leadership focuses on thinking critically about how leadership is worked out in early childhood practice. Underpinned by empirical research from across the early years sector, a range of practitioner profiles and voices are used to illustrate, examine and discuss the core features of the leadership within process in action. Particularly useful for graduate early years leaders, and all students of early childhood education and care practice, this book includes valuable material that will challenge thinking about the development and professional identity of leaders in early years provision in the twenty-first century."

Gill Goodliff, Department of Education, The Open University, UK

"This book has the potential to do for nurseries what Michael Fullan's work did for schools, to re-affirm the moral heart of leadership. Often omitted from accounts of early years professionalism, an attitude of care is advocated as the central characteristic of leaders. At the same time, Clark and Murray challenge the traditional explanation for this attitude amongst practitioners in terms of female nurture, presenting it instead in non-gendered terms as a function of ethical character and commitment. With their concepts of catalytic agency, reflective integrity and relational interdependence, the authors provide an intellectual justification for something that many practitioners have long known intuitively, that early years leadership calls for a marriage of both mind and heart."

Dr Geoff Taggart, Lecturer in Early Years, University of Reading, UK

Contents

Acknowledgements

We would like to acknowledge all the research participants whose passion has inspired us and informed our thinking.

List of tables and figures

Tables

Figures

Foreword

The importance placed on leadership in the early years has gained considerable ground in recent years as governments have invested in the sector both in terms of levels of provision and the qualifications of staff, with an emphasis on increasing the proportion of graduates. The roles and expectations placed upon the early years in contemporary society and the drive to give children the best start in life has brought an external spotlight on what might be achieved for young children whereas in the past the early years was all too often dismissed as straightforward by those outside the field – probably principally because of the age of children it serves.

In fact from within early years is one of the most complex fields of social, cultural and educational practices: the wide range of professionals involved, the focus on interagency working, the importance of children's emotional well-being, learning and cultural participation and the principle of working with children and their families and communities, each serve to highlight the complexity and demands of early years practice. Such insight means that collectively we must not import uncritically from elsewhere, nor bow to top-down approaches: rather the sector must continue to explore its own needs, rights, challenges and ethics. A pioneering spirit has never been far away in early childhood – it is a quality that safeguards this field and makes space for re-thinking past practices and developing new: this book takes the foreground in such an approach.

Reconceptualizing Leadership in the Early Years provides an opportunity to consider how leadership in the early years has been conceptualized in the past and to reflect on leadership in the early years context now. The literature on early years leadership has not been extensive and in practice there have been confusions about the balance of management and leadership (Dunlop 2008). In numbers of early years settings there is an expectation of effective teamwork whilst administrative and management duties might be enacted, for example, by the head of the school where a nursery class is situated, or by a charismatic head of centre: in such situations understandings about leadership may be ambiguous. If the discourse of leadership in early childhood has been confused, it is not without history – but too often is has relied on models of leadership imported from other sectors and disciplines that consequently fail to take account of the responsive and relational pedagogies that are a mark of ethical practices in this sector. Exceptions to this have been the growing body of work emanating from New Zealand, from Finland and from England. Much too has been written in recent years about professionalism in early childhood – this is also a diverse concept in a sector where many types of professional are represented: this diversity also brings complexity (Dalli 2005).

Much of the literature has reached a conceptualization of leadership in the early years that considers skills for leadership to include collaborative management styles and distributed leadership (CoRe Final Report 2011). The recommendations of the CoRe report include the need across Europe to build leadership capacity: linking to this, the report asserts the importance of linking theory and practice: 'Building *leadership* capacity is a crucial precondition for ensuring strong, reciprocal and equal relationships between theory and practice' (p. 50). Further, Urban, Vandenbroeck, and Peeters, the authors of this report, assert that the complexity of the early years field calls for 'the same level of attention and investment in leadership capacities as is now common in school leadership' (p. 51). They see the English model of '. . . introducing and supporting the role of *early years professionals* as potential *change agents* (as) one example of a national approach to building leadership capacity' (p. 51). It is a pleasure to find a book that acknowledges these journeys and offers a new presentation of leadership for early years whilst being grounded in long held values-based early childhood practices including, for example, that care and education are inseparable (Dalli 2006) and that professionalism is important.

Whilst Urban, Vandenbroeck, and Peeters emphasise the importance of relationships between theory and practices, Muijs *et al.* found that most of the leadership research in this area was more narrowly informed by theorizing about early childhood contexts and qualities and avoiding the broader field of research studies (Muijs *et al.* 2004 in Dunlop 2008: 11). If leadership is going to be fit for the many aspects of early years practices, it will need to draw on this wider field. Leadership capital will build when it is well informed: psychology, sociology, the law, education, health, social policy are just some of the theoretical fields from which the diverse and complex early years sector can draw. Rory McDowall Clark and Janet Murray use this wider view to address issues of gender, management, self-concept and self-agency, learning, pedagogy and practice as well as to consider the values that inform early years work. In this way readers are offered specific field knowledge embedded within a range of work that complements the diversity which encompasses inter-agency working, continuous professional development, the gendering of leadership, the ethics of care, work with parents and the implementation of curriculum.

It is good to see such a well thought through approach to leadership in the early years. The authors have used their research skills, academic experience, knowledge and engagement with practice to produce a reading experience that will encourage but not intimidate practitioners who seek to meet the challenge of making the best possible provision for young children through active reflection on, and in, their practice. For newcomers to theoretical argument I would recommend starting with the preface, followed by the case study chapters in Part 2 and to then make use of these to unlock the theoretical work that supports and is embedded in the new model of leadership in the early years that is presented in Part 1! The practice examples make the theoretical arguments clear and accessible.

Reconceptualized leadership serves not only as a theoretical model for leadership and thinking about leadership but as a practical process and guide – as social practice: each element supporting the next. My own thinking about leadership had moved beyond the charismatic, the shared and the distributive, to ideas of mutuality and 'leadership embraced' – I have therefore particularly enjoyed the juxtaposition of words used to reconceptualize and inspire new thinking, inner knowing and confidence – catalytic agency, reflective integrity and relational interdependence – all elaborated in the pages ahead and all promoting leadership within.

Aline-Wendy Dunlop, Emeritus Professor,
School of Education, University of Strathclyde

References

CoRe (2011) *Competence Requirements in Early Childhood Education and Care, Final Report*. University of East London, Cass School of Education and University of Ghent, Department for Social Welfare Studies. (Public open tender EAC 14/2009 issued by the European Commission, Directorate-General for Education and Culture.)

Dalli, C. (2005) *Reflecting on professionalism in early years teaching: Relationships, responsiveness and curriculum*. Guest Lecture, University of Strathclyde: 6 September 2005.

Dalli, C. (2006) Revisioning love and care in early childhood: constructing the future of our profession, *New Zealand Journal of Infant and Toddler Education*, 8(1).

Dunlop, A-W. (2008) *A Literature Review on Leadership in the Early Years*. Glasgow: Learning and Teaching Scotland. Available at www.ltscotland.org.uk/images/ leadershipreview_tcm4-499140.doc [accessed May 2012].

Muijs, D., Aubrey, C., Harris, A. and Briggs, M. (2004) How do they manage? A review of the research on leadership in early childhood, *Journal of Early Childhood Research*, 2(2): 157–60.

Preface

For most of the twentieth century early childhood education and care (ECEC) was considered peripheral to the real business of education; a concern for practitioners and parents but with little relevance to the rest of society. By the 1990s this perspective had begun to change so that now, in the second decade of the twenty-first century, ECEC is widely recognized as an integral aspect of modern societies. The importance of the foundations laid down in children's early years and the subsequent impact of these on their later health, educational success and overall life chances is acknowledged not only by practitioners and academics but also by politicians, economists and policy makers who increasingly look to early years provision from an instrumentalist perspective as a way to address social and economic issues.

The increased focus on early years provision and a belief in the redemptive power of childhood institutions to address pressing social concerns has turned the spotlight onto leadership in the sector. The need for effective professionals to take a lead in developing provision that can support the well-being of young children and their families is axiomatic and a number of texts have examined aspects of early years leadership (Moyles 2004; Muijs *et al*. 2004; Rodd 2006; Siraj-Blatchford and Manni 2007; Aubrey 2011). Certain themes emerge from these authors such as the current scarcity of data and evidence that can contribute to an understanding of early years leadership; the need to develop leadership potential and capacity from within the sector; and the nature of leadership in a multiprofessional context. In particular, such texts have been important in drawing attention to the complexity of leadership against the background of contemporary emphasis on interagency collaboration which makes the early years distinctive – a factor which leadership texts deriving from the field of education fail to address.

This book seeks to add to the debate. We hope to respond to calls for more experiential data by building a bridge between the theory and practice of early years leadership, between praxis and paradigm and between rhetoric and reality. We believe the implications of recent moves to professionalize the workforce have been insufficiently examined in relation to leadership and that this offers a unique opportunity to reconceptualize leadership and develop a new paradigm more suited to the specific circumstances of the sector. We also contend that the assumption that leadership derives from specific named individuals, a legacy of educational leadership models, is unhelpful and limiting. Our paradigm of *leadership within* offers a way of conceptualizing leadership

which can be applied and practised by practitioners at any level of an organization and offers models which meet the specific characteristics of the early
childhood field.

This book is divided into three parts. Part I examines the current context
and sets out our proposed paradigm of *leadership within* which is then explored
in relation to actual practice in Part II. In this way, the first part of the book
may be regarded as more discursive where we justify our intent to reframe early
years leadership whereas the second part concentrates on applied theory and
illustrates how these concepts can be identified in practice. A final chapter in
Part III summarizes the ideas explored in the book and considers the implications for sustainable leadership development in the sector.

Recommended reading is given at the end of each chapter in Part I so that
readers can pursue points further and broaden their knowledge. In Part II, we
have offered instead a number of reflective prompts to extend understanding,
stimulate further debate and support the reader in applying these ideas to their
own practice. We write from an English perspective because that is the working
context of the practitioners and children's services with which we are involved.
To enable wider understanding of this context we have included a glossary of
terms. Each term featured in the glossary appears in **bold** when first used.

Part I begins with a chapter outlining a broad overview of different theories and notions of leadership to show how concepts and understanding have
developed in recent years. This sets the context for consideration of leadership
on a meta-level, drawing out the implications of different approaches and clar-
ifying where their emphasis lies. This enables readers to place their own beliefs
and values into a broader framework against accepted models and perspectives
and demonstrates the need for a new paradigm for early years leadership.

Chapter 2 examines the context of the early years sector in the UK to
consider the circumstances which underpin our call to reframe early years
leadership. Recent changes in policy are identified and current influences on
the sector noted. Ideas about leadership of early years settings are considered
including the conflation of leadership and management and the suggestion
that early years leadership is a particularly 'female' attribute.

In Chapter 3, we set out our argument for a new model of leadership for the
early years. We term our paradigm *leadership within* because it is leadership which
emerges from within the social practice of organizations, groups and communities and is not dependent on personhood or positions of authority. We believe
that *leadership within* operates on two levels – as inner leadership, concerned
with self-awareness and personal agency and as diffused leadership (leadership
spread throughout an organization). We have identified three specific features of
leadership within, namely *catalytic agency, reflective integrity* and *relational interdependence* and in this chapter each aspect is set out and explored.

Part II of the book examines the features of *leadership within* in more detail
by analysing and evaluating a range of leadership profiles to demonstrate how

the paradigm relates to actual practice in the field. The authentic voices of early years practitioners from a wide variety of backgrounds, experiences and settings provide opportunities to examine leadership as a process rather than an individual characteristic or behaviour. The profiles cover a broad range of circumstances; male and female practitioners at every level from managers to generic nursery assistants as well as parents and governors. The spread of workplaces includes private, voluntary and maintained settings but no schools have been included because we wish to focus clearly on ECEC and not blur the boundaries with school leadership. The data which inform our thinking have been drawn primarily from individual interviews (Chapters 4, 5, 7 and 9) but also include material from reflective accounts (Chapters 6 and 9) as well as participant observation on the part of one of the authors (Chapter 8).

Chapter 4 features Sarah, an Early Years Professional (EYP) and manager of a voluntary pre-school. As the only practitioner qualified above level 3 in her setting, Sarah can sometimes struggle to support her colleagues' proactive development of their practice. The opportunity to visit Reggio Emilia in Italy encouraged her to share her enthusiasm with others in order to extend the provision and pedagogy of her setting. This account illustrates the *catalytic agency* which is fundamental to *leadership within*. Sarah's example highlights the central importance of passionate care as a driver for professional practice and the exercise of leadership (Murray in press), which is notable in all of the practitioners featured here and an integral element of *leadership within*.

In Chapter 5, we consider the relationship between gender and leadership. The fact that the early years workforce is overwhelmingly female has often been used to argue that this results in a distinctly gendered leadership approach. We would suggest that such an explanation is unhelpful and that a nurturing leadership style stems from early years values rather than gendered behaviour. Nonetheless an examination of male experiences adds an important dimension to our examination of *leadership within* because both Tom and Daniel, the two male practitioners interviewed in this chapter, work in a sector where their gender makes them unusual. These two men demonstrate how *reflective integrity* is fundamental in their approach to their different roles and the leadership that they display.

Chapter 6 illustrates the third aspect of *leadership within*, namely *relational interdependence*. June's role in a private nursery entails her working with other practitioners, parents and outside agencies and all these relationships are interdependent. As deputy and room leader, June's leadership does not lie in telling others what to do but in her self-awareness and sense of being one among others who work together to enhance practice.

Chapters 7, 8 and 9 illustrate the three features working at a diffused level. Chapter 7 interviews two different practitioners working in Children's Centres in the same area. Like Sarah in Chapter 4, both Nina and Marie have visited Reggio Emilia and this has impacted on their practice and how they see their roles. The wider community engagement of the Reggio approach has inspired them to use similar values in their own settings and thus demonstrate leadership through diffused *catalytic agency*, which then has an impact throughout the community.

In Chapter 8, the issue of values, which must be central in the consideration of leadership, comes to the fore as the aspect of *reflective integrity* working at a diffused organizational level is considered. Two situations are explored: a serious safeguarding case which ended in a child being taken into care and a change of direction for the centre as a whole. Both of those situations instigated profound soul searching on the part of staff and governors to examine tensions and dilemmas which raised questions concerning the relationship between espoused values of all participants. This chapter illustrates the need for reflective practice to be built on a foundation of integrity.

Relational interdependence operating at a diffused level is the topic of Chapter 9. In this chapter, the personal development stories of two parents are used to demonstrate how leadership capacity was generated through their involvement in a family centre, thus contributing to an increase in overall human capital.

The final chapter draws together the learning from these 'varied journeys into leadership' (Aubrey 2011: 61) and considers the implications of this paradigm of *leadership within*. The connection between leadership and learning is highlighted in relation to leadership development. The dearth of development opportunities is identified in much of the literature (Muijs *et al.* 2004; Siraj-Blatchford and Manni 2007; Aubrey 2011) but this is frequently conceived as specific training for people holding identified positions of authority. We believe that by changing the focus from leaders to leadership the potential capacity of a professional workforce may be more fully realized and diffused within the community. *Leadership within* offers the opportunity for a broader community, including practitioners at any level, to engage in leadership practice.

Aubrey (2011) has suggested that opportunities for sharing experiences of other leadership situations offer a foundation for more focused consideration of leadership which can aid reflection and support agency for change. We hope that the profiles presented here can give rise to wider debate about the potential of all members of an organization to be involved in the process of leadership. Early Years Professionals have been used as exemplars within many of the leadership profiles because both authors are involved in different ways in the work of a major provider of EYPS (Early Years Professional Status) programmes and because the development of this status has drawn attention to non-hierarchical leadership. The paradigm of leadership proposed has wider applicability, however, as is evident in Chapters 8 and 9, so that the issues, challenges and opportunities represented here offer insights and can be utilized in a broader educational context.

PART I
Reframing leadership

1 A paradigm for leadership

This chapter will examine the usefulness of paradigms and definitions in assisting understanding of leadership. It will provide a broad overview of the development of leadership thinking up to the present day and consider whether our thinking needs reframing to meet the needs of the twenty-first century and the particular context of the early years sector, commonly referred to as **early childhood education and care (ECEC)**.

A paradigm as a mental frame

A paradigm is a useful construct for framing our thinking about a topic – in this case, leadership. It provides a mental frame or lens through which we can examine ideas and create an approach to researching the experience of leadership. The intention is that it casts some light on our understanding of the topic, when seen within that frame, and creates conceptual tools to support exploration. It can be likened to a picture frame in that it should draw attention to what is inside and should complement its subject, yet the choice of materials and design can alter the way in which the subject is viewed, changing the emphasis of some of the features in the eye of the beholder. It is important, therefore, to remember that a paradigm cannot and should not attempt to be definitive but can allow us to see an old subject from a new perspective.

A paradigm is an academic device which provides:

- a value position or perspective giving a world-view, stance or lens through which to examine the topic;
- characteristics, features or concepts which make the paradigm distinctive;
- boundaries and scope to examine the topic in different situations and contexts, using the paradigm features to develop understanding;

- models which can be derived from the above ideology to use in practice.

The test of a paradigm is its usefulness when applied in the real world. It requires theory and practice to be brought together in a way which can support making sense of the lived experience. A paradigm provides a perspective for research which makes the value base and world-view explicit and can, in turn, influence the adoption of particular research tools. By implication, therefore, the limitations of the paradigm should be apparent for scrutiny. It may have temporal and cultural limitations in illuminating the topic under considera- tion but this is not necessarily disadvantageous when working with such a complex and wide-ranging topic as leadership.

Defining leadership

Leadership has been a topic of research and study for centuries and yet there is no generally agreed definition (Avery 2004; Gill 2006; Western 2008). In fact, there are well over a thousand definitions demonstrating that whilst it is a common term it has diverse meanings (Gill 2006). For such a complex concept, there is a danger of reductionism if a narrow view is taken, yet a danger of being too amorphous if a broad definition is adopted. So, leadership 'remains elusive and enigmatic, despite years of effort at developing an intellectually and emotionally satisfying understanding' (Avery 2004: 3).

Definitions tend to reflect the approach taken to the subject and the context in which it is being studied and therefore definitions vary in emphasis from seeing leadership as something individual (based on authority or influ- ence) or more generic (as a group process). It has been variously defined in terms of traits or competencies, or as a process, relationship or construct (Gill 2006). Western (2008) highlights the diverse and subjective nature of leader- ship when he says it can have multiple forms and meanings and can be found in many different places, so it may be considered individual, collective, or a process depending on where we are looking. What is common is that leader- ship operates in the realm of human relations.

The search for a generic definition is not our task and, indeed, may not be helpful as the notion of leadership needs to embrace a multitude of human and organizational contexts and allow examination of the complex nature of human relationships. Leadership can take place among friends, with peers, in formal positions, informal groups, within or outside of an organization and with or without management responsibilities. It can emerge in an instant, such as an emergency, or it can be a way of being as a person or a group. The notion of leadership needs to embrace this potentially endless range of situations and be responsive to change and capable of adaptation over time, allowing historical, cultural, social, political and experiential influences to modify interpretations of what leadership means.

The complexity of the notion of leadership is part of its nature and should not be avoided but it is probably too limiting to see it only as a notion. If leadership is also seen as a phenomenon, then the world of experience and interpretation of that experience becomes part of what it is. Exploration of that experience becomes a valid and necessary part of a research paradigm seeking to develop leadership understanding. Inclusion of the experiential dimension is important for leadership learning, drawing attention to what is occurring in the process of leadership and in the behaviours and responses of those who are involved or affected. Attention to the experiential dimension makes leadership inherently reflective and reflexive, enabling change and adaptation individually or collectively. 'Critiquing one's personal leadership practices and the leadership encountered within our organizations and workplaces, liberates us from being trapped within the dominant normative discourses and enables emancipatory change to occur' (Western 2008: 6).

When viewed as a social construct, leadership is normative. It is influenced and shaped, at least in part, by the values, beliefs and assumptions of the culture in which it operates and the underlying dominant political and philosophical discourses, both historical and current. Post-modernism highlights the need to consider pervading influences and authority and the way in which they affect general perceptions and expectations of leadership. Western (2008), however, argues that post-modernism underplays personal agency, having a tendency to see the human players as passive, dominated and subjugated to social norms, rather than active and creative. He calls for means to liberate thinking from social, political and cultural constraints, placing more emphasis on autonomy and the ability of individuals and groups to be self-determining and creative, allowing reconstruction and interpretation of leadership in new ways.

These world-views enable us to understand how, as a social construction and experienced phenomenon, leadership can be a broad and changing notion. It has no fixed identity because it is in a constant state of deconstruction, interpretation, and reconstruction. The absence of an agreed definition of leadership frees up possibilities for revisioning within any specific set of circumstances and influences. We will not, therefore, attempt a generic definition but intend to use this freedom to explore leadership within the specific set of circumstances that is early childhood education and care (ECEC). This context is developed further in Chapter 2.

Paradigms of leadership

Ideas about leadership have developed in an historical perspective with particular characteristics and emphases which can be traced through a timeline from the nineteenth to the twenty-first century. These have been broadly categorized into paradigms of classical, transactional, visionary and, most recently, organic theories which demonstrate their distinguishing features, concepts and ideology (Avery 2004). While a paradigm can be a useful construct for study to aid interpretation and understanding, a single paradigm is unlikely to be manifested in a pure form or in a single historical period, simply because it is part of a process of developing thinking and examining experiences. The variety of different paradigm characteristics can help us understand the range of leadership approaches which can operate contemporaneously within the same organization and within individuals, depending on context and situation. So it is probably more apt to see the development of ideas about leadership as a spectrum rather than a continuum, with a chameleon-like ability to adapt and blend colours to fit the environment and context.

As well as evolving in a social, historical, cultural and political context, paradigms of leadership embrace theories which have arisen out of studying a particular situation, for example business, public service or education, and therefore emphasize different elements and values relevant to the nature and purpose of that organizational sector. Consequently, paradigms differ in their focus depending on where they situate leadership – in the person, position or process. When leadership is located in *personhood*, the traits, attributes or competencies of a leader and the leader/follower relationship are central. In *positional* leadership, power, authority, role and hierarchy will feature with the emphasis on the leader within organizational systems. When leadership is seen as a *process*, interactions and reciprocity of relationships will be the prime focus of attention. The interplay of ideas relating to person, position or process in leadership theories are not mutually exclusive but the emphasis gives those theories a character which can be broadly placed within current paradigms of leadership, depicted in Table 1.1. This table represents the four main paradigms developed to date, demonstrating how they can be characterized by the way in which leadership is exercised; what focus is dominant; and where leadership is situated.

The first three of these paradigms (classical, transactional and visionary) have different emphases but still largely situate leadership with the *leader in a designated position*, exercising leadership through power, systems and the strength of personal traits or behavioural competencies.

Classical and visionary ideologies might seem like stark contrasts in the way leadership is exercised, yet both focus on the personhood of the leader with the emphasis moving from inherent traits to personal and behavioural qualities exhibited in the ways of working which inspire others to work towards the organization's goals. Leadership of this nature is quite commonly, but not exclusively, found in flat hierarchies where the authority or influence of a single person, usually the positional head, is strong; consequently there is a merging of meaning between leadership and management. Flat hierarchies are not uncommon in small ECEC settings where a single person overwhelmingly has major

Table 1.1 Leadership paradigms

Leadership paradigm	Exercised through	Focus	Situated in
Classical	Command and control	Leader	Personhood
	Power and authority		Position
Transactional	Managerialism	Task	Position
	Mechanistic tasks	Systems	
	and rewards	Leader/follower	
		Superiority/dependency	
Visionary	Inspiration	Leader/follower	Personhood
	Charisma	Mission	Position
	Authenticity		
	Transformation		
Organic	Relationships	Sustainability	Process
	Participation	Capacity development	
	Distributed, shared or		
	collective responsibility		

responsibility for provision. There is sometimes a significant difference in qualifications and expertise from the other staff members who look to the titular lead person to provide all the leadership, whether by command or inspiration. Lambert (2003: 423) suggests: 'Timeworn assumptions have persuaded us that leader and leadership are one and the same' and therefore expectations and beliefs about effective leadership are focused on the skills, qualities and dispositions of the designated managers. Traditional views of leadership as a single positional leader are remarkably durable in public perception. Avery (2004) found that the idea of command and control and the authoritative leader continues to be a persistent model dominating popular thinking about leadership even though leadership literature has moved more towards visionary, emotion-based and distributed models (Day 2004; Harris 2004; Harris 2008). Whatever individual style of leadership the positional lead person adopts, this focus on the leader as a single individual in a management position is neither suitable for long-term sustainability of the organization nor ultimately well suited to the nature of early years work where responsible and reciprocal relationships are central.

Transactional leadership also focuses on the positional or designated lead role in a structure with hierarchical superiority between leader and followers. There is a differing emphasis, however, on management of systems and procedures to exercise leadership and fulfil organizational purposes (Harris *et al.* 2003). The focus is on efficiency and the breakdown of tasks to individual performance, where success is measured against targets, outputs or standards. Transactional leadership developed from the rationalist–scientific management perspective in the 1970s and can be considered bureaucratic, with the focus on task management, delegation and performance measurement. This is in contrast to ideas which emerged in the 1980s and 1990s where achieving organizational goals was seen to require leaders to create a culture of followers with a shared mission; a period which saw the emergence of the visionary (transformational) paradigm. This does not, however, mean that the influence of scientific management and transactional leadership is over. Eacott (2010), citing Kanigel (1997), suggests that it is so embedded we hardly recognize it, using the concept of 'best practice' as an example of a simplistic means–end approach to finding what works in order to replicate it. The attempt to define and use standards or traits as a basis for assessing professional competency is another example of using rationalist logic in the belief that a single set of criteria can provide the means to achieve the desired end. The problem with reducing leadership to a set of standards, traits or behaviours is that it takes no account of the social context or the interplay of human relationships.

The ECEC sector is not traditionally highly bureaucratic so it is generally less pertinent to talk about hierarchies. While some providers base their organization on positional authority for management and commercial considerations, the essential nature of the business is to provide care for the well-being and education of young children. This requires consideration of shared and effective practice which is heavily reliant on relationships and interaction, elements which are not readily amenable to standard measurement. The idea of leadership as an allotted function of management, where a leader assumes a central designated role, conflates concepts of leadership with the position of the 'leader'. It also creates categories of leader and follower which carry notions of superiority/inferiority and therefore power and authority. This implies that leadership is done to others rather than being something which people can participate in, which is not to deny that nominated leaders, unequal power and authority exist, but that as a concept of leadership it does not offer sufficient inclusivity. It encourages too much emphasis on the personhood and attributes of a leader and is insufficiently broad-ranging.

When examining current paradigms of leadership, it is important to bear in mind that many theories draw their understanding of leadership from the business sector. Public sector and educational leadership literature developed to counter the predominance of the technical–rational business perspective in order to reflect better the values, purposes and intrinsic nature of services ultimately aimed at furthering the well-being of society. This body of literature places greater emphasis on a sense of service and shared mission (Fullan 1999), values and relationships (Sergiovanni 2001) and emotional and ethical leadership practice (Day 2004; Harris 2004). A body of educational leadership literature and research has developed which sees leadership as not entirely explained in what leaders do or their characteristics but containing an important affective dimension. It is this dimension which has been attributed with the facility to enable change and development by providing certain emotional conditions conducive for change (Day 2004). The idea of emotional intelligence has been very influential and Goleman *et al.* (2002) produced a list of attributes of the emotionally intelligent leader. The emphasis, once again, is on the individual and the personhood of leadership and unfortunately, in this case, the leader is also presupposed to be male! We need to place less emphasis on 'the leader' to be able to conceptualize 'leadership' better and to lose a gender orientation in thinking about leadership to avoid stereotypical thinking.

Visionary and transformational paradigms of leadership gained popularity in educational circles in the early twenty-first century when the drive for school improvement was seen to require strong and effective school principals who could communicate a vision and create a sense of shared mission in followers (Day *et al.* 2000). Studies of successful leaders showed how they effected change in working cultures through transforming the needs and aspirations of the individual or group to align with organizational purposes, a move away from self-interest to collective interest (Avery 2004). In some cases, this idea of leadership is akin to the heroic leader but operating through emotional effects between leader and followers. Theories in the visionary or transformative paradigm often identify leadership as working through charisma, inspiration or modelling an explicit and recognizable set of values (such as ethical or authentic leadership). Eacott (2010: 271) suggests this line of thinking has arisen from studies focusing on what successful school heads do, which has led researchers into normative theorizing resulting in 'a proliferation of adjectival leadership theories each prescribing their own specific ideal model for effective leadership'. Such 'how to do' models of leadership return to an unrealistic idea that there could be a 'one size fits all' prescription for leadership. This does not do justice to the complexity of the phenomenon of leadership or the variety of leadership contexts, neither does it provide tools for supporting reflection on leadership practice which is where active knowledge-creation about leadership is generated. Theory needs to support reflection on practice rather than provide a template for action (Spillane *et al.* 2004).

Transformational leadership perspectives gave rise to theorizing leadership as a collaborative culture based on positive relationships (Harris *et al.* 2003). Sergiovanni (2001) suggested that superheroes were a thing of the past and that leadership in the twenty-first century would be exercised through developing communities of responsibility. A change of emphasis in the literature, from the task to the process of leadership, is becoming evident (Lambert 2003; Gill 2006) and Lambert (2003: 424) suggests that 'those who are redefining leadership situate it in the processes among us, rather than in the skills and dispositions of a leader'. While there remains a persistent focus on the 'leader' as a designated position with an underlying leader/follower perspective, most recent theories are moving towards group-based, participative and shared leadership. These are described as within the organic paradigm and include the idea of distributed leadership developed primarily from educational leadership literature (Spillane *et al.* 2001; Harris 2008). Theories in the organic paradigm have grown out of concern for lasting improvement arising from culture change but with an emphasis on sustainability of change and leadership capacity. There has been growing recognition that sustainable improvement cannot be achieved by a single leader. Alma Harris suggests 'there is a powerful argument for looking at alternative ways of leading, looking for competing theories of leadership and challenging the orthodoxy that equates leadership with the efforts of one person' (Harris *et al.* 2003: 1).

In developing a new paradigm for early years leadership, we need to bear in mind that popular perceptions are durable and bring expectations about ways of working, relationships and responsibility that may need to be challenged if we are to develop greater understanding and take our thinking about the experience of leadership forward. The cultural and historical context and nature of ECEC services are generally, although not entirely, different from both business and public service, and while there is much in common with educational purposes the ECEC sector is multidisciplinary and has a differently constituted proportion of public, private and voluntary providers. It should be expected, therefore, that current paradigms may have limited application and a new paradigm needs to have clear relevance to the whole workforce and visible application to a range of work situations for greatest impact. As Rodd (2006: 11) identifies, 'Research into leadership has been criticized as being too focussed on exploring what leaders do (Mitchell 1990) and the attributes they possess . . . [these models] do not offer insight into the complex process of leadership, which is multifaceted and based on reciprocal relationships (Morgan 1977).' Relationships are central to leadership generally and especially pertinent to the nature of work in the early years. So disaggregating the notion of positional leader or a single individual from the concept of leadership can be useful and Lambert (2003: 424) suggests that 'as a concept separate from, yet integrated with leader, leadership stands as a broader notion, a more encompassing idea'.

It is this more encompassing idea that we shall explore further in this book with specific application to ECEC. In considering a new paradigm of leadership for early years we wish to avoid equating leadership with the idea of a 'leader' because of the danger of reducing leadership to traits or norms of behaviour and also to remove assumptions that leadership refers only to particular individuals in a designated position. We will focus more on the *process* of leadership, which moves the focus away from *who* is doing the leading to *how* leadership is taking effect. It directs our attention away from concerns about *what is led* (people or organizations) and towards *leadership with or within* (collective or personal orientation and endeavour). We will do this by examining and applying three new paradigm features through a number of leadership profiles and scenarios in Chapters 4–9.

Leadership for the twenty-first century

While there is much to be learned from the vast array of leadership theories encompassed within paradigms which have evolved over a significant period of time, there is a constant need for re-examination within the perspective of current experiences and changing conditions. Each historical period has its own social, economic and technological developments which affect how people and organizations work and what is considered conducive to working effectively. These in turn influence expectations, requirements and interpretations of leadership. The twenty-first century is characterized by globalization and technology creating more open and immediate access to information and quick communication. There is more emphasis on the rights of individuals and groups and more facility to make their views known and contribute to consultations. This is changing the ability of consumers, stakeholders and staff to be more immediately involved in and influence the business of an organization, breaking down or reducing hierarchical boundaries. In some fields of work, there are also significant changes in the nature of relationships where contact is remote or rarely face to face. In ECEC, the focus on rights and communication is a modern emphasis with greater involvement of stakeholders in service provision. The service, however, is essentially immediate and face to face between practitioners, children and families in a shared physical space, so relationships remain central and more traditional. Clearly, there are also remote and technological communication methods involved but they do not characterize the essential nature of the service.

Recent literature on business, public service and educational leadership have some common perceptions about the challenges of the twenty-first century related to globalization, technological development, the rapid pace of and demand for change, work intensification and issues of sustainability (Avery 2004; Hargreaves and Fink 2006; Bennis 2007; Harris 2008; Western 2008). Greater distribution and decentralization of knowledge are bringing expectations of immediate and open communication and a demand for transformation and improvement. Social and cultural changes increasingly emphasize the need for a more inclusive and participative perspective of leadership and the complexity and demands of modern working life make the heroic individual leader an untenable model. There is recognition that leadership needs to be present across and throughout an organization to be sustainable, where agency for change can be released and a greater sense of involvement can be generated among the workforce. This reflects a more equal, complex and diverse society where common responsibilities are being encouraged for social, environmental, and educational well-being.

The twenty-first century is seeing the emergence of a paradigm of leadership described variously as 'organic' (Avery 2004) or 'ecological' (Western

2008) that is less focused on the single leader, less about command and control and more about building networks, collaborating, acting ethically and responsibly through a shared leadership process. It draws on the language of human ecology, examining human relations and interactions with each other and the environment, and emphasizing interdependence, connectivity and sustainability. It is non-hierarchical, flexible and responsive, enabling leadership to emerge at any level in an organization, wherever the appropriate knowledge, expertise or initiative occurs and with the ability to identify and act on challenges and opportunities. The collective and ethical nature of responsibility ensures that the leadership process has checks and balances and is orientated towards commonly negotiated goals (Avery 2004). The organization is seen as a living system interconnected to a wider environment which needs to take the long view for sustainability (Hargreaves and Fink 2006; Harris 2008). This is particularly appropriate to the ECEC sector where practices and investment are intended to have a long-term return in the child and society's future.

The notion of distributed leadership falls within the early development of the organic paradigm. Distributed leadership, as all leadership theory, is open to different interpretations in different contexts and sometimes still retains a leader/follower distinction and terminology which sees leadership as management authority bestowed from the top down, distributed to maximize use of time, knowledge and skills. The emphasis is on the interactions between leaders and followers seeking to release expertise at local level, enabling responsive and responsible action. Some interpretations of distributed leadership have more emphasis on the potential for collective leadership and broad-based participation if structural obstructions are removed (Harris 2008). They call for empowerment and involvement rather than delegated spheres of responsibility. Alma Harris (2008: 152) believes that 'Future leadership will be concerned with *participation and relationships* rather than leadership skills, competencies or abilities. Future leaders will be spread across the organization, and will constantly nurture and fuel new knowledge, new ways of knowing and new ways of doing.'

Western (2008) argues that a critical theory approach is needed to achieve this, providing a framework to support examination of leadership practice so that it can be freed from dominant ideas, opening up new ways of thinking and options for change. He argues for an emancipatory paradigm which enables a greater sense of individual and collective autonomy with the ability to effect change.

Reframing thinking

In conclusion, there are calls for a new paradigm to reframe thinking about leadership which is more suited to the needs and issues of the twenty-first century. A more inclusive perspective is developing which invites involvement and shared responsibility across a community or organization. This enables participative leadership models to emerge which embrace the idea of connectivity between people and their environment. A critical framework is needed to bring theory and practice together, releasing creative thinking about leadership to bring about new ways of working. The paradigm shift we pursue in Chapter 3 contains three concepts to support critical thinking about leadership in the particular context of ECEC, encouraging a focus on active participation and relationships. These concepts characterize the paradigm of *leadership within*, namely catalytic agency, reflective integrity and reciprocal relationships.

Further reading

Gill, R. (2006) *Theory and Practice of Leadership*. London: Sage Publications.
This book provides a comprehensive examination of the history of leadership theory and explores different perspectives and paradigms.

2 The context for leadership in the early years

This chapter examines the background and character of the ECEC sector in order to set a context for appraising ideas of early years leadership. It sets out recent developments in the UK as well as influences from elsewhere so as to understand how these have impacted on practice and provision in the field. An account is given of the evolution of current ideas about leadership in the sector and the major messages from this work are outlined. The implications of the highly gendered nature of the early years workforce are considered and the subsequent issues this raises for concepts of leadership are evaluated. In particular the suggestion that leadership in early years settings draws on specifically female attributes is challenged as a notion which ultimately undermines the professionalism of the sector. The topics raised in this chapter underpin our argument for why a new model of leadership is necessary and what such a paradigm can offer.

The early years context and character

The evolution of early years leadership has been many years in the making. The role of adults has always been considered one of the most crucial factors in enabling young children to flourish and Friedrich Froebel, commonly thought of as the founding father of the early years tradition, developed training centres early in the nineteenth century for young women to be taught the necessary skills to work in kindergartens. Froebel's name has been associated internationally with the development of early years expertise ever since, although his emphasis on young women as the only appropriate practitioners has left a legacy which continues to affect the sector today (Ailwood 2008). By the early decades of the twentieth century Susan Isaacs was in the forefront of initiatives to train specialized nursery teachers who would have an understanding of the particular social and emotional development of young children. Although training from the time of Froebel onwards was rigorous and professional, the focus was entirely on child development and interaction with the child.

In Britain, early years education and care (ECEC) remained very much the Cinderella sector (Willis 2009) throughout most of the twentieth century. Despite the Plowden Report (CACE 1967) advocating the benefits of nursery education for children over 3, there was little political will to resource provision outside statutory requirements. Lack of government investment meant that what provision did exist was developed in a very piecemeal fashion with limited statutory provision supplemented by the **private, voluntary and independent (PVI)** sector. By the end of the 1980s there was a dire need for action and co-ordination and the Rumbold Report *Starting with Quality* (DES 1990) called for closer integration of different strands of provision. It also identified the need for a clear lead from central government in setting a national framework, a move which could be seen as the beginning of accountability for the sector. In addition the Rumbold Report drew attention to the need for well-qualified, graduate staff to implement all of this, a proposal reaffirmed soon afterwards in the *Start Right* report (Ball 1994).

The early years sector really began to move to centre stage with the election of the New Labour government in 1997. The National Childcare Strategy (DfEE 1998) outlined plans for better quality, more accessible childcare and increased places for 3- to 4-year-olds. Unprecedented investment in the field followed as childcare became a vital part of the wider political agenda, supporting the economy and a drive to encourage parents, and women in particular, to return to work (Baldock 2011). After being returned to government for a second term New Labour laid out further plans for development in the Ten Year Strategy, *Choice for Parents, the Best Start for Children* (HMT 2004) and these were updated during a third term in office (HM Government 2009) as the provision of nursery places continued to expand. Over this period a parallel drive towards devolution in Britain offered new opportunities for policy development as each country in the United Kingdom was starting from a low baseline of provision (McDowall Clark 2010).

Such dramatic growth of early years provision has not been without criticism. In particular, concern has been raised about tensions between the push for a greater quantity of childcare places and the maintenance of quality (Ball and Vincent 2005; Sylva and Pugh 2005; Penn 2007; Pugh 2010). These issues are particularly pertinent because of the implications of a rapidly growing private sector in which only 3 per cent of staff are graduates in contrast to 40 per cent within maintained settings (Baldock *et al.* 2009). The Childcare Act (DfES 2006) provided legislation to support the Ten Year Strategy, introducing a number of measures intended to address these concerns by ensuring comparability between very diverse systems. These included the introduction of common curriculum frameworks and revised inspection procedures unified under Ofsted in England or its equivalent elsewhere. Devolution has enabled the separate nations of the UK to respond according to their own perceived priorities, for instance the Welsh Foundation Phase Framework (WAG 2008), the ***Early Years Foundation Stage (EYFS)*** in England (DfES 2008), *A Curriculum for Excellence* in Scotland (Scottish Executive 2005) and the Northern Ireland Foundation Stage curriculum (CCEA 2006), all of which have different emphases and cover different age groups. This has opened the door for increased professional dialogue and debate in the sector.

Over the period of New Labour's administration there were purposeful attempts to integrate early years education and welfare traditions to tackle the persistent split between education and care. This had been identified within the original National Childcare Strategy in 1989 but was given added impetus after the death of Victoria Climbié by the Laming Report (Laming 2003), which informed the ***Every Child Matters*** green paper (DfES 2003) and ultimately the *Children Act* (DfES 2004). *Every Child Matters* suggested that multiprofessional and interagency co-operation should be at the heart of effective service delivery, and 'joined-up' services to enable this to happen were made statutory under the new Children Act. Joint working arrangements for the delivery of children's services were established between education, health and social services at local authority level under **Children's Trusts** and this integration was also evident at national level with one minister and government department responsible for children, young people and families. The **Common Assessment Framework (CAF)** was introduced to support multiagency working and **Integrated Children's Centres** were established in the most deprived areas providing a model whereby a whole range of family support services could be made available in one central location in response to local needs. This was progressively expanded under the Childcare Act (DfES 2006) with the intention of providing Children's Centres in every community. All of these initiatives pointed to a need for effective and purposeful leadership in the sector.

Underpinning many of these moves was a political agenda of reducing social exclusion and family poverty. The goal of improving families' welfare and health increased the emphasis on working in partnership which is evident in *Every Child Matters*, the EYFS and the Childcare Act. This was reiterated in the *Children's Plan* (DCSF 2007), which recognized that, while 'Governments do not bring up children – parents do', nonetheless some parents may well need additional support if their children were to reach the five outcomes of *Every Child Matters*. The underlying objective behind these measures was a focus on early intervention to prevent problems from developing rather than waiting to react at a later stage when they had become more critical. For this reason 'child protection' became reframed as 'safeguarding children' and there was a drive to embed services for vulnerable children within universal provision.

In order to be able to respond to the challenges of so many reforms and the increased expectations that accompanied them, the government recognized the importance of investing in the professional development of the children's workforce (Miller and Cable 2008). The *Children Act* (DfES 2004) initiated workforce reform and in 2005 the **Children's Workforce Development**

Council (CWDC) was established to develop an integrated qualifications framework. Recognition that the specific challenges of integrated working in the early years required a new kind of practitioner was evident in the development of new professional roles, in particular the **National Professional Qualification in Integrated Children's Centre Leadership (NPQICL)**, parallel to the head teachers' qualification, and **Early Years Professional Status (EYPS)**, parallel in status to teachers. There have been a number of issues raised in connection with these new roles, not least the difficulties of maintaining equivalency of status in the absence of comparable pay scales, but nonetheless the professional standing of work with younger children is long overdue and must be welcomed (McDowall Clark and Baylis 2010). While these are English initiatives, similar moves are taking place in other nations within the UK, for instance the early years organization NIPPA (Northern Ireland Pre-school Playgroup Association) is committed to developing a graduate early years workforce on the European pedagogue model (Walsh 2007).

Current influences on the sector

The initial promotion of good quality nursery provision, as advocated in the Rumbold Report, was driven by the principles of the early years tradition (Bruce 2005). In more recent years developments have been underpinned by an empirical evidence base derived from extensive long-term research into the circumstances which best support young children's learning and development. The **Effective Provision of Pre-school Education (EPPE)** project (Sylva *et al.* 2004) investigated the impact of pre-school provision on 3000 randomly selected children and has been progressively extended to follow those children through to a stage just beyond their GCSE year (Sylva *et al.* 2010). Findings indicate that outcomes for children are improved when they attend settings which are led by graduate staff who support and extend thinking processes through a stimulating programme which balances education and social development.

The EPPE report has had a very significant impact on early years provision; it has underpinned policy initiatives such as the Ten Year Strategy, the EYFS and EYP standards. In addition it has led to other research such as the REPEY report, which researched pedagogy in those settings identified as effective (Siraj-Blatchford *et al.* 2002) and ELEYS, which examined leadership in the sector (Siraj-Blatchford and Manni 2007). The EPPE findings have since been reinforced by the Millennium Cohort Study (Mathers *et al.* 2007), which confirmed that quality is significantly enhanced in maintained settings and those with a qualified teacher. A recent report (Mathers *et al.* 2011), set up to evaluate the impact of specialized early years graduate professionals, reached similar conclusions, showing that EYPs provide 'added value' to settings in terms of overall quality over and above gaining a graduate.

Ongoing empirical research such as this justifies the very considerable public expenditure on early years provision over recent years and the drive to raise qualifications of the workforce. Against a background of concern about the long-term effects of child poverty, Springate *et al.* (2008) have drawn attention to the potential of high-quality provision and appropriate intervention to improve life chances and 'narrow the gap' between the most disadvantaged children and their peers. Their review emphasized the significance of skilled, qualified professionals and the involvement of parents in their children's learning. The significance of the home environment was also highlighted in the EPPE project, and the importance of partnership with parents to support children's holistic development, a key theme in previous government policy, remains clearly visible in current initiatives (DFE 2011). This emphasis on the parent as caregiver and first educator, however, can also be in tension with government initiatives to encourage more parents back into the workforce (Pugh 2010).

International influences have also had a bearing on current practice in early years, in particular the impact of the **Reggio Emilia** approach and growing interest in forest schools. The inspiration of Scandinavian forest schools has acted as a stimulus in encouraging much greater use to be made of outdoor learning spaces and highlighted the importance of 'enabling environments' (DfES 2008). Reggio pre-schools also regard the environment as a vital part of children's learning, referring to it as 'the third educator' (Rinaldi 2006). In particular the Reggio approach emphasizes 'the child as a subject of rights and as a competent, active learner, continuously building and testing theories about herself and the world around her' (OECD 2004:12). The prominence given to children as active participants in their learning stresses relationships as fundamental to children's development and reinforces the need for skilled practitioners who, acting as co-learners and researchers, facilitate and support children's thinking. The way in which inspiration from the Reggio approach has influenced local practice is explored in Chapter 7.

Contemporary approaches to early years education and care are thus built on the idea of trust in the child's ability to select and initiate his or her own activities in joint ventures with qualified professionals who are proficient at resourcing environments to nourish and sustain this. This requires skilful experts and Moyles *et al.* (2002) recommend that there should be an expectation for adults to engage in the same metacognitive processes that we encourage in children. They suggest that practitioners' inability to articulate their own practice and its theoretical underpinnings 'may put a significant constraint upon effective pedagogical practices' (2002: 3). Such an expectation calls for a different type of leadership, pedagogic leadership, which can bridge research and theory (Aubrey 2011).

While it has been gratifying that ECEC has achieved a position of prominence after 'years of indifference' (Baldock *et al.* 2009), at the time of writing there are many changes poised to affect the sector, the implications of which are still uncertain. Failure to elect an outright government in the British general election of 2010 resulted in a coalition government with no clear mandate. It is evident that a different political ideology will change the emphasis on universal services for all children towards more targeted provision; this is already indicated in modifications to the Sure Start remit and changes in the 'language' of early childhood services such as the term 'help children achieve more' in place of the five outcomes of *Every Child Matters* and a return to the concept of 'child protection' rather than 'safeguarding'. Other moves include a review of the EYFS framework (Tickell 2011) which will bring about changes from September 2012. Although this has been cautiously welcomed for reducing the long list of expectations for pre-school children and simplifying paperwork, there are also concerns about the inappropriateness of assessing young children against learning goals and the emphasis on the early years as preparation for school as opposed to being valid in its own right (Open EYE Campaign 2011). In addition to the Tickell Review, recent policy direction in respect of young children has been informed by the coalition government's response to the Field Report into poverty (Field 2010) and the Allen Report on early intervention (Allen 2011). Before the general election Baldock *et al.* (2009) suggested that, whichever party was in power, the expansion of child-care provision would be likely to continue and with it an emphasis on family support, cross-agency co-operation and inclusion. This direction has been confirmed by a recent government statement pledging continued investment to support targeted, family-based early intervention to enable children from disadvantaged backgrounds to catch up with their peers (Teather 2011). Pugh (2010), however, warns that future developments are likely to be affected by uncertainty about funding as public expenditure is squeezed. She also points out that an unintended consequence of requirements to 'narrow the gap' is pressure to skew an otherwise broad and balanced curriculum to meet goals which are not appropriate for all children. All of this makes it more important than ever that the early years sector has strong leadership able to adapt to changing circumstances and advocate for young children and their families.

Developing models of leadership in the early years

Jillian Rodd (2006: 7) has argued that if early childhood is to fully realize professional status, equivalent to that of similar or related occupations, then we must 'nurture and train individuals who will emerge as leaders from within the profession'. She regrets the fact that leadership 'continues to be an enigma for many early childhood practitioners' (2006: 5). However, Muijs *et al.* (2004: 158) point out that early years professionals 'view themselves first and fore-most as educators and child developers' and it is probable that the very things that draw people into a career working with children in the first place are likely to be at odds with many of the traits and characteristics which are commonly associated with leading. Such a perceived contradiction can make many people reluctant to take on nominated leadership roles in the first place or else to fail to recognize what they do in their own roles as leadership (McDowall Clark and Baylis 2011).

Muijs *et al.* (2004) suggest that a result of early years practitioners being viewed primarily in their role as educators is that research about leadership in the field has been limited and largely anecdotal. They bemoan the dearth of real evidence, particularly when compared to the extensive research literature on school leadership. This complaint was also echoed by Siraj-Blatchford and Manni (2007), whose research report *Effective Leadership in the Early Years Sector (ELEYS)* investigated the characteristics of leadership displayed in those settings which had previously been identified as providing effective pedagogy (Siraj-Blatchford *et al.* 2002). Siraj-Blatchford and Manni regret that 'Due to the paucity of evidence based (i.e. non-anecdotal) literature that is available related to the leadership and management of early years settings, the authors were forced to consult leadership and management literature associated with both primary and secondary schools'(2007: 7–8).

That such an extensive body of literature and research had arisen within the statutory school sector over the previous two decades is not to be wondered at because this was a period when the spotlight came to bear on education in a similar way to the recent focus on early years provision. The introduction of a National Curriculum, increased monitoring of teachers and auditing of school results through league tables caused widespread upheaval as the government sought to make Britain internationally competitive in a globalized market place. Traditionally head teachers used to be particularly skilled or ambitious teachers who were promoted to lead a staff team; new expectations of schools meant that management and business skills became essential. It is now taken for granted that head teachers of large schools work in a similar way to executives of large corporate organizations in a context far removed from the classroom. This required a whole new conceptualization of the role of educational leaders and recognition that teaching skills were not sufficient; specialized training was also necessary. In a similar way, Siraj-Blatchford and Manni (2007: 11) suggest that there is a 'misconception that one's success as an early years staff member will naturally translate into a successful leader'. Although recognizing that NPQICL has paralleled the head teachers' leadership qualification, they draw attention to the thousands of early years leaders whose training needs are not being met.

The origins and nature of school leadership meant that the focus was largely on transformational concepts of leadership (see Chapter 1), with an emphasis on managing change. Such a focus continues to be important within the early years sector because of the importance of multiprofessional inter-agency working (Anning *et al.* 2006; Aubrey 2011). There are many different routes to change, however, and it may come about through a variety of styles of leadership.

The models of leadership most commonly found in the educational literature are visionary leadership and distributed leadership (see Chapter 1). Schools are naturally hierarchical institutions; regardless of aspirations to run democratically they are nonetheless under the supervision of a head teacher and control emanates from the top. Visionary or transformational leadership which rests on an image of the leader as a charismatic personage inspiring followers and transforming their organization may have a place in schools but it is not a paradigm which comfortably fits the early years sector, where Rodd suggests most practitioners are 'averse to being in a position of dominance' (2006: 16). We do not consider it to be a helpful paradigm in an early years context because such a concept of leadership is largely dependent on the personal characteristics of one individual and this can create an element of passive dependency, or at the very least over-reliance, on a single leader.

Distributed leadership (Bennett *et al.* 2003), wherein leadership is spread within an organization, is an attempt to move away from the dominance of a solitary individual and to share, or distribute, leadership throughout a community. Although recognizing that there are various interpretations, Bennett *et al.* suggest that distributed leadership is characterized by the openness of boundaries so that expertise is dispersed among the group. This is clearly a much more democratic model than one in which a single individual assumes control and is actively promoted by the National College of Schools Leadership (NCSL 2007).

Distributed leadership is also a feature of the ELEYS study, which concentrates on 'concrete leadership behaviours rather than . . . beliefs' (Siraj-Blatchford and Manni 2007: 7). The authors identified specific characteristics of effective early years leadership practice, which they outline as follows:

- identifying and articulating a collective vision, especially with regard to pedagogy and curriculum;
- ensuring shared understandings, meanings and goals: building common purposes;
- effective communication: providing a level of transparency with regard to expectations, practices and processes;
- encouraging reflection: which acts as an impetus for change and the motivation for ongoing learning and development;
- commitment to ongoing, professional development: supporting staff to become more critically reflective in their practice;
- monitoring and assessing practice: through collaborative dialogue and action research;
- building a learning community and team culture: establishing a community of learners;

- encouraging and facilitating parent and community partnerships: promoting achievement for all young children.

Although the ELEYS study recognized that leadership and management are separate functions and that a balance must be struck between them, nonetheless leadership is envisaged as stemming from an individual who is in a position of authority in charge of others. Such conflation of leadership and management roles tends to permeate the literature in the field (Moyles 2004; Rodd 2006; Aubrey 2011), although Rodd points out that leadership can be exercised at different levels. She suggests that there is a need to 'unravel' what is understood as leadership so as to enable more 'grass roots' practice to emerge (Rodd 2006: 19).

Jillian Rodd was the first to consider leadership specifically within the field of early years, pointing out the unique features of this multidisciplinary sector and the resulting flexibility required. Her text on *Leadership in Early Childhood,* first published in 1994, has been reprinted several times over a period in which increased accountability and expectations have fuelled a demand for strong leadership in the sector. Rather than focusing on leadership behaviours and attempting to identify a specific leadership style, Rodd draws on examples from a range of international practitioners to identify the strategies which leaders adopt in their work. Since then others, such as Janet Moyles and Carol Aubrey, have continued to examine the sector to identify the particular issue of leadership in the early years.

Moyles's research project (2004) studied heads of 16 different early years centres encompassing private, voluntary and independent as well as maintained settings. This resulted in a tool called ELMES-EY (the Effective Leadership and Management Evaluation Scheme for the Early Years), intended to enable managers to self-evaluate their effectiveness and identify their training needs. Although recognizing that leadership and management are not discrete roles, Moyles positions them within one nominated authority figure to develop a typology of skills across four different areas:

- leadership skills;
- management skills;
- professional skills;
- personal characteristics.

We depart from this focus on management and nominated leaders to view leadership diffused throughout the organization or community and manifested within processes rather than skills and characteristics.

Carol Aubrey and her colleagues also studied a number of early years leaders from 12 different settings using a grounded theory method (Strauss and Corbin 1990). Their intention was to explicate the actions and interactions arising from the rapidly changing English context and identify how the role of early childhood leaders has become more challenging due to interrelated policy initiatives resulting from the ECM agenda. Aubrey (2011: 170) suggests that while there is a clear need for early childhood leaders to distribute leadership throughout the setting 'it is unlikely that one model or a single approach can be appropriate for such a diverse sector'. She draws attention to the added difficulties of multiagency, multiprofessional agendas which have increased the range and complexity of expectations but at the same time offer opportunities for networking and collaboration that can enable new models of leadership to emerge.

While both of these empirical studies focus on the English context, there has been a growing interest in early years leadership elsewhere in the UK (Dunlop 2005) and beyond (Oberheumer 2000; Kagan and Hallmark 2001; Nivala and Hujala 2002; Ebbeck and Waniganayake 2003) as the profile of the sector continues to rise on the global stage. Despite increased focus on the topic there remains considerable ambiguity about what leadership entails within the very specific context of the early years and a tendency to focus largely on the positional lead. Ebbeck and Waniganayake (2003) bemoan this lack of clarity, which they suggest is a consequence of changing circumstances and the resultant evolution of roles and responsibilities. They call for a paradigm shift and, like Siraj-Blatchford and Manni (2007) and Aubrey (2011) borrowing from education and school leadership, suggest that a distributed leadership model might be the most appropriate way forward.

But isn't it just a 'female' thing?

Notions of leadership within the early years sector are additionally complicated by its strongly gendered nature – indeed Osgood (2010) has argued that ECEC may be seen as lacking in professionalism precisely because it is deemed 'hyper-feminine'. Cultural stereotypes of women as caring and nurturing means that they have always tended to be concentrated in the social welfare, health care and education professions. Women's responsibility for 'emotional labour' (Hochschild 1983) and attention to the needs of others is reinforced by their characterization as gentle and altruistic. Early childhood is a particularly gendered occupation because it conflates such deeply entrenched definitions with the maternal role and this has particular implications for the consideration of early childhood leadership. Muijs *et al.* (2004) point out that the extent to which women occupy leadership roles combines with the complexity of the field in establishing leadership in the sector as wholly different to that in schools. Such female domination, however, creates difficulties in itself as some commentators use this as an explanatory device and seek to locate leadership practice within gender-specific behaviour (Shakeshaft 1989; Hall 1996).

Nonetheless, gendered analyses of leadership have contributed perspectives from which to consider different leadership approaches of particular relevance to early years (Scrivens 2002).

The impact of second-wave feminism in the last few decades of the twentieth century ensured that gender has become an important variable in social science research; in particular a search for specific gender 'differences' has dominated empirical studies (Cameron 2008). Such a focus has the result of amplifying any perceived differences and creating an impression that gendered behaviour is somehow 'natural' rather than a cultural and social phenomenon. The emphasis has been on identifying and then explaining any variations in approach between male and female leaders – so women's greater use of collaborative and participatory leadership styles (Shakeshaft 1989; Hall 1996) is generally accounted for as a consequence of their supposed enhanced emotional intelligence. Conversely, Reay and Ball (2000) explain these supportive behaviours as arising from women's greater likelihood of being trapped in lower status jobs. Certainly working in the early years sector has long been seen as a lower status occupation than teaching in schools (Hargreaves and Hopper 2006) and the lesser material rewards help to contribute to a lack of men entering the profession; however, seeking to explain early years leadership through the predominance of female practitioners runs the risk of confusing cause and effect as well as devaluing professional attributes of co-operation, collaboration and connectivity. Dunlop (2008) argues that it can be precisely those characteristics of good early years leaders which parents value, such as emotional warmth, which serve to reinforce ideas of early years as less rigorous than other sectors of education.

The association of women with the early years is strongly connected to the expressive characteristics which Dunlop (2008) suggests parents value so highly. Although the raised profile of the early years sector has generally been welcomed, there is also concern that increased accountability could overwhelm this caring dimension and result in more technical and instrumentalist approaches (Osgood 2006b). Such approaches are generally associated with more masculine styles of leadership so this has implications with regard to working relationships with colleagues. Henderson-Kelly and Pamphilon (2000) have suggested that traditional models of leadership embodying masculine values and attributes do not easily transfer to the early years field and therefore women professionals are developing new styles of leadership, based on collaboration and dialogue, which are more appropriate to the sector. In addition uneasiness has been raised that government initiatives to expand childcare provision by promoting entrepreneurial approaches encourage a masculinized, business culture and so could endanger the ethic of care (Osgood 2004). All this might suggest that the 'ethic of care' (Gilligan 1989) is primarily a female prerogative and that the gender of the workforce is one of the most crucial aspects to consider in relationship to leadership.

We would argue that gender is not a particularly helpful concept in analysing early years leadership because it runs the risks of misconstruing early years values as gendered values. This is reinforced by certain feminist perspectives which maintain that women are intrinsically more socially adept, emotionally literate and collaborative in their nature (Hochschild 1983; Gilligan 1989). There is an easy slippage between such essentialist concepts of women and the maternal discourse that pervades ECEC (Ailwood 2008). From an essentialist perspective, women are seen as somehow 'nicer' than men: they are 'softer', more 'cuddly' and, in short, display attributes that result in a more humane style of leadership. However, the danger of using such dichotomies as analytical frameworks is that they are limiting and preclude, rather than open up, possibilities for interaction. If the affective domain is associated with the female in contrast to the rational, male domain, then there is a great loss of potential; quality early years practice must seek to combine both affective and rational ways of working. Furthermore, essentialist views that regard a predisposition to nurture others as a female attribute endowed by nature do women no favours. The assumption that co-operation and collaboration are 'natural' female traits devalues the skills and proficiency evident in such conduct and ultimately undermines the professionalism of female leaders. Although certain behaviours may have traditionally been associated with one gender or the other this does not preclude all leaders from exercising and displaying a broad range of qualities. Aubrey (2011: 2) warns against the danger of 'too closely associating characteristics of leadership with masculine or feminine values and qualities' and suggests that this 'leads both to stereotyping women and alienating nurturing men'. While leadership must be value-based (Murray 2009), it is a mistake to identify these values as specifically female ones and although women themselves may wish to believe that they bring a more humane and nurturing approach to leadership, Wajcman (1999) found no evidence to support this notion. The issue of gender is explored further in Chapter 5.

Reframing early years leadership

Recent years have witnessed substantial transformation in the field of early years amounting to a virtual revolution. There is no reason to believe that the pace of change is likely to slow down in the future. The implications of such developments are that leadership will become increasingly important and must be the practice of many rather than the few so that organizations can foster and sustain quality practice. Early years leadership needs to be pervasive to be able to make sense of rapidly shifting events and policy and to cope with the complexity of changing circumstances. Any theory of leadership needs to take account of changing expectations, to be fit for purpose and itself be capable of withstanding change.

This chapter has considered the current early years background to contextualize our search for a leadership paradigm, or conceptual framework, that can be philosophically aligned with early years principles and values. Although we have argued in Chapter 1 that it is unnecessary, indeed unhelpful, to attempt to define leadership, this does not preclude us from attempting to theorize it. Indeed, we cannot avoid doing so. In everyday life, we continuously speculate and create explanations for what we see going on around us so that 'theory' is implicit in our most commonplace assumptions. For this reason Eagleton (1990) asserts that 'all social life is in some sense theoretical' and it is impossible to remain outside theory. If this is the case then it is incumbent on us to systematically examine leadership in a theoretical manner so as to be able to act consciously and with deliberation.

Whereas existing theories, such as those explored in Chapter 1, are a helpful starting point, they are insufficient to explicate the particular circumstances of ECEC. The huge variety of different settings and organization across the maintained, private, voluntary and independent sectors complicate the task. Such complexity, combined with an expectation of working across traditional professional boundaries, require that we pay heed to collaborative ways of working and theories of leadership that embrace teamwork and co-operation. While we would agree with Henderson-Kelly and Pamphilon (2000) that there is a pressing need to reframe and develop new models of leadership appropriate to the sector, we would dispute that these models are necessarily female ones. Instead we argue from a more inclusive perspective that leadership should be built on affective values (Moyles 2001; Osgood 2010) and that while leaders need to be emotionally intelligent (Goleman 1996) this is a characteristic that can be, and is, demonstrated by both male and female practitioners and by the many, not the few. A feminist perspective is important in challenging the discourses which continue to represent childcare as an instinctive female aptitude and the subsequent lack of value such skills engender in both esteem and recompense. It is important, however, not to misconstrue values arising from the early years ethos as essentialist female ones.

We would also challenge the notion that leadership is a subset of management – a legacy of business-focused models which is still apparent in much of the literature – and instead offer a paradigm in which leadership may emerge from anywhere within an organization. The strategic leadership which is an aspect of management is quite different to pedagogic leadership and identifying leaders of practice (CWDC 2010) is another way in which ECEC provision is set apart from other organizations. All settings need to be effectively managed but this is quite different from leadership and conflating the two functions not only confuses the perspective but also precludes many practitioners from being able to demonstrate leadership. We suggest that leadership can emerge from anywhere within a setting but that it requires consciousness and criticality arising from reflection. It is these issues that we explore in the paradigm of leadership which is set out in the next chapter.

Further reading

Pugh, G. and Duffy, B. (2010) *Contemporary Issues in the Early Years*. London: Sage Publications.
Gives a broad overview of the context and background to ECEC policy and practice.

Rodd, J. (2006) *Leadership in Early Childhood*, 3rd edn. Maidenhead: Open University Press.
This seminal text draws on a range of perspectives from across different countries to give an insight into early years leadership through the ways in which individuals work.

3 A new paradigm for early years leadership

This chapter examines the features that have impacted on our thinking as we set forth our paradigm for early years leadership. In particular, we would emphasize the location of leadership within the processes of working together rather than within individual personhood or the hierarchy of an organization. The distinction and relationship between intrinsic and extrinsic leadership (Gill 2006), that is, between inner leadership and that which is collective and organizational, is also considered. Building on these ideas we propose a new paradigm of leadership – *leadership within* – which is non-hierarchical, has an inner dimension and operates as a diffused process in the organization or setting. This paradigm has three key features – *catalytic agency, reflective integrity* and *relational interdependence*. The final part of the chapter examines each of these features in turn.

Personhood and process of leadership

Leadership, as any other social phenomenon, is a socially constructed concept and needs to be interpreted according to the social and cultural context in which it occurs. Ideas about leadership can be expected to change over the course of time in response to wider historical and political influences as is evident in the trajectory of theoretical accounts of leadership discussed in Chapter 1. As Starratt (2007: 175) points out, '[k]nowledge in any society is always in the process of being constructed, deconstructed and reconstructed because of changing circumstances, new technologies, new power relationships in society.' This does not mean that ideas about leadership are necessarily determined solely by the prevailing political or theoretical discourse as they are capable of being actively shaped by the people engaged in a given situation or circumstance. The nature of leadership as a 'situational, socially constructed and interpretative phenomenon' (Hujala and Puroila 1998: 8) enables new interpretations to be developed that can better suit the particular circumstances of ECEC. Nonetheless, ideas about leadership are inevitably affected by enquiry and debate taking place in broader public arenas and concerns which characterize the contemporary period. Over recent years there has been increasing acknowledgement that the idea of the formal leader at the helm, steering the ship, as the principal locus of leadership is limiting and unsustainable in the complex, diverse, technological era in which we live (Avery 2004; Bennis 2007). More inclusive notions of leadership are developing which see leadership as a process; something that happens collectively rather than something which a leader does to others (Lambert 2002). In the search for theoretical alignment that fits ECEC values and ethos, this is a particularly useful notion because it shifts the focus away from formal authority and places it instead on group processes and collaborative action.

Such a change of focus requires system transformation and new ways of thinking about leadership (Kaser and Halbert 2009). It needs an environment which encourages involvement and inclusivity to enable leadership to flourish across and throughout the organization. In the context of school leadership, Lambert (2002) argues that there is a need to develop leadership capacity within the whole school community as a shared undertaking. She sees leadership as a reciprocal and participative process embedded in the context and culture of an organization which produces energy and purpose. It is both a right and a responsibility in which '[e]veryone has the right, responsibility, and ability to be a leader' and the way leadership is defined influences how people engage in it (Lambert 2002: 37). 'Therefore leadership can be seen as a systemic rather than an individualistic construct; an inclusive and democratic concept promoted by the social environment' (McDowall Clark in press).

The view of leadership as a process underpins ideas of distributed leadership which have been particularly influential in the literature about schools and educational leadership (Spillane 2006; Harris 2008). This has led many writers to suggest that distributed leadership may provide a promising theoretical basis for ECEC (Ebbeck and Waniganayake 2003; Siraj-Blatchford and Manni 2007; Aubrey 2011). While distributed leadership has some relevance, most of the research base has depended on individual school leaders and we would argue that this is insufficient as a perspective that fits the particular circumstances of early years provision. Some features of distributed leadership, such as the shared responsibility of learning communities (Harris 2008) and an emphasis on concertive action (Gronn 2002), are relevant and useful as they break down historical boundaries of leadership. Nonetheless, distributed leadership is sometimes too closely connected with senior management distribution of responsibility for delegated areas or projects, resting on assumptions of leadership as something that can be 'distributed' or given out rather than an embedded and self-generating process. This is too specific to the school community and does not provide a sufficiently developed and inclusive framework for theorizing ECEC.

Rather than seek to apply existing theories of leadership to such a specific context as early years in an attempt to find the 'best fit' (Handy 1993), we would suggest it is more important to start with the practice. What is needed is a new paradigm that can provide a framework for thinking differently about leadership and a vocabulary which enables discussion and debate to take place about what this concept means for early years practice. We wish to move leadership thinking away from personhood and position because these create dependencies on individuals, reduce collective responsibility and do not promote a sense of capability or leadership participation across the organization. Whilst acknowledging that the formal leader has a significant role to play, we wish to divert thinking from the positional role or function of a leader because of the dangers of conflating leadership with management and the distraction of what formal leaders do rather than how they work with others. Early years practice is based on co-constructivist pedagogy which provides a way of working and learning as adults and children through dialogue, purposeful action, interaction and reflection. Change, which is at the heart of the learning process, is also closely connected with leadership (Brown and Posner 2001). The link between leadership and learning has been well established and is particularly relevant to organizations with learning as their core business and common purpose. We propose, therefore, to examine early years leadership as related to a process of learning shown in the manner of how a setting or individual works. We will look at leadership in two dimensions: inner leadership (within the individual) and diffused leadership (within the collective working of the organization). This paves the way for consideration of how early years leadership might productively be reconceived by means of our paradigm of *leadership within*.

Inner and diffused leadership

Leadership takes place at individual, team and organizational levels. It is both interpersonal and intrapersonal (Nupponen 2006). For leadership to be consistent and sustainable it needs to be present in the processes and culture of the organization rather than reliant on individuals. Yet individuals help to make it happen through their actions, behaviour and interactions. Consequently there has been increasing attention in leadership literature towards the creation of organizational culture, identity and shared mission. Most theories place this as a responsibility driven by the formal leader requiring them to have particular qualities to encourage followership (Kelley 1992). Research into early years professionalism (Moyles 2001; Osgood 2010; Simpson 2010; Murray in press), however, has consistently demonstrated that there exists a strong sense of moral purpose or social mission at the heart of early years professional identity and motivation, irrespective of formal position. The existence of such a professionally innate driving force or motivational mission encourages individual responsibility, prompts personal agency and provides inclination to support initiatives with a compatible, common purpose. For ECEC, this common purpose has a social and ethical dimension: to act in the best interests and further the education and well-being of young children and their families. The strength of common purpose in the sense of early years professional identity is indicated in the terms most commonly used by practitioners to describe it, such as 'passion', 'ethic of care', 'desire', 'love of children' (Moyles 2001; Rodd 2006; Osgood 2010). This core of 'moral purpose' (Fullan 1999: 11) provides motivation for working individually and collectively for the benefit of others; this is not unusual in public service but some view this as potentially oppressive, making early years practitioners vulnerable because of the sense of selfless service or 'emotional labour' it produces (Osgood 2010; Taggart 2011).

We would argue, however, that the passionate care at the heart of early years professionalism provides the raison d'être for working with children and brings commitment and persistence to keep the child at the centre of thinking. It is a source of great strength and supports resilience to manage change and overcome obstacles. It is most often described as wanting to 'make a difference' and shows a belief in personal agency to effect change. The widespread presence of this motivating force among early years professionals demonstrates that 'principled leadership is potentially present in the whole team' (Murray 2009: 23) and if released could create a sustainable basis for leadership. Passionate care for furthering the well-being of children is an ethically active, professional orientation, not a domestic concept of care. When coupled with critical and reflective pedagogy, it provides guidance for professional practice and behaviour (Taggart 2011). For the individual, it creates an inner guide of personal professional expectations and, if made explicit in a setting or organization, it can create a powerful sense of community and common purpose. This is the essence of inner and diffused leadership.

Inner leadership

Gill (2006) identifies leadership as having two dimensions: extrinsic (provided by others) and intrinsic (arising from within ourselves). For Gill, intrinsic leadership is leadership of self, displayed by having a vision, knowing what to do, being self-aware and self-driven. If this is taken at face value there could be a danger of single-mindedness, relentless ambition or missionary zeal so we would argue that self-awareness is particularly important as a checking mechanism. Also, we suggest that self-leadership needs to be orientated by a worthwhile purpose greater than the individual to be constructive. It requires an inner direction to sustain self-motivation and moral purpose, providing agency to take action for a greater goal. We prefer the term 'inner leadership' as it prompts self-reliance and self-organization to tackle problems or obstacles and persist with individual effort. External control is not necessary or desirable, as motivation is sustained internally – it is *self*-control (Covey 1992). To operate effectively a sense of inner security and self-responsibility is fundamental. Development of self-confidence is part of this to spur moving into unfamiliar ground, meeting challenges, coping with uncertainties and being open to new possibilities. This is based more on a belief in the worthiness of the vision (in principles and values) rather than as personality traits. Personal integrity and the drive for improvement become self-fulfilling goals with a natural concern for continual personal learning and developing expertise.

This links naturally with reflective practice which includes personal evaluation and seeks feedback to provide an inner accountability. Research with candidates for Early Years Professional Status (EYPS) found inner leadership, as described above, to be characteristic of successful candidates (Murray in press). As one expressed it, 'It's about taking responsibility for what goes right and wrong and learning from it.' Inner leadership encourages making a personal contribution, recognizing and using strengths and working with others to best effect in pursuit of common purposes. What is required therefore is an organization with inner leadership emerging from within every quarter, diffused throughout. We are aiming for early years settings where inner leadership produces active agents of change and where diffused leadership provides empowerment and capability to make this happen collectively.

Diffused leadership

Organizations cannot operate without the people within them working collectively at some level but people experience and interpret organizations differently so that it might be argued that 'organizations are the creations of the people within them' (Bush 2003: 113). The culture or identity of the organization is the product of interactions and practices so that a community of practitioners displaying inner leadership produces a dynamic organization with a clear mission and purpose. For ECEC, both inner and diffused leadership are firmly rooted in passionate care for young children and their families, bringing the cognitive and emotional aspects of leadership into one holistic concept.

Lambert (2002) places shared responsibility for mutual learning as central to her model of leadership and part of her framework for school improvement. She suggests broad-based participation in leadership brings learning and leadership together in professional practice. Both leadership and learning are in this way concerned with the process of growth and development. Professional learning goes hand in glove with children's learning and as both are concerned with social responsibility for children and their families they naturally align with leadership learning. In organizations with learning as their core purpose, leadership requires no distinction between organizational and pedagogical purposes as leadership is concerned with learning and improvement. Dunlop

(2008) suggests that leadership in the early years sector has much in common with pedagogy as they both involve reciprocal relationships and shared construction of knowledge.

The notion of diffused leadership describes the potential for the pervasive presence of this mutual responsibility in early years settings. The ways and means to achieve diffused leadership participation may vary according to the size, complexity and context of the setting and its potential can be affected by the approach and conceptual understanding of the formal management. If leadership, like learning, can be seen as central to early years practice, it becomes part of everyone's purpose and way of working.

Although diffused leadership requires common purpose and works on shared construction of knowledge, it does not deny difference, ambiguity or conflict. It has a learning orientation and therefore welcomes challenge, reflection, diversity and multiple perspectives. The advantage is that multiple perspectives can be expressed and heard and become part of the shared experience of knowledge construction.

Features of the paradigm

Based on the two dimensions of inner and diffused leadership, we propose a new paradigm of leadership – *leadership within* – which is non-hierarchical and recognizes that leadership can come from anywhere within an organization or a setting. This paradigm locates leadership as a process which is catalytic, reflective and reciprocal and therefore has three key features – *catalytic agency, reflective integrity* and *relational interdependence*. Although these features are interconnected and work together they may also be considered as separate and distinct elements so while we shall now examine them individually as discrete components we will also draw attention to how varying aspects interrelate (see Figure 3.1).

Catalytic agency

A major feature of the paradigm of leadership from within is the aspect of *catalytic agency*. This refers to a willingness to take action and practitioners' recognition of their own individual ability to make a difference. The term agency means more than simply taking part; it implies a proactive involvement which makes an identifiable impact. It is important that early years professionals recognize their shared accountability for high-quality practice – accountability to parents, carers, colleagues, the wider community and, above all, to the children themselves. This evidently requires being prepared to make choices and assume responsibility, so it entails deliberate, sustained action and personal agency.

Personal agency becomes *catalytic* when it is used to bring about broader change. A catalyst is a term used to describe a substance which can be added to

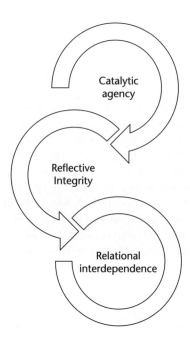

Figure 3.1 The three interweaving features of *leadership within*

a mixture to bring about internal change and create something new. Therefore catalytic agency refers not just to willingness to take personal responsibility for one's own actions, but suggests a purposeful intent to use this as a force for improvement and to bring about change.

Catalytic agency cannot be exercised without autonomy – the opportunity to be self-regulating and to determine one's own actions. Fromberg (1997) identified autonomy as one of the essential attributes of professionalism and something which differentiates a professional from someone who is merely doing a job. This paradigm of leadership does not rest on authority or power but nonetheless requires a certain level of autonomous responsibility in order to make independent decisions and achieve objectives. Provided they are able to work in a self-determining manner then every early years professional can demonstrate leadership from within.

Catalytic agency should be a consequence of *reflective integrity* and the questioning and challenging of practice in order to improve provision and ensure that it is meeting the evolving needs of young children and their families. Any practitioner can criticize the organization of a setting or the practice of others but it is in the willingness to adopt a proactive stance in relation to improvement where leadership from within can be identified. Individuals take on responsibility for both personal actions and organizational behaviour, recognizing and seizing opportunities for improvement and modification. This continuous evaluation of the broader environment is not a matter of change for the sake of it but acknowledgement that improvement and development should be an ongoing process; an attitude which Margy Whalley has described as 'constructive discontent' (2007). Early years professionals who question and challenge practice in a constructive manner and then use this as a basis to bring about positive change are using their personal agency as a catalyst to improve provision within their setting.

Being prepared to make a difference and bring about change requires a certain level of courage and resolution. Many people are nervous about change and become anxious when the familiar circumstances in which they are used to operating are altered. It is important that the need for continuity and stability does not become an excuse for retaining unhelpful or inappropriate practices but, by the same token, neither can it be assumed that change is always necessarily a good thing. Sometimes change may be imposed simply because somebody wants to make their mark or it may come about as a knee-jerk reaction to new initiatives from elsewhere. Any change must always be balanced against the needs of the children and the organization as a whole. Contemplating the metaphor of a catalyst as a chemical substance can be helpful in considering how change comes about – while one wants to avoid a mixture so inactive that it becomes stagnant, adding too much of a catalyst could lead to an unstable and explosive mix which would be equally undesirable. The leader from within who exhibits catalytic agency recognizes the importance of taking small, incremental steps to bring about gradual evolving improvement at a manageable level. So this paradigm of leadership moves attention away from an end product to a focus on the processes at work instead.

Such catalytic agency works through the power of influence rather than dominance and authority. If leadership from within is to be regarded as a process then it is essential that it is a shared journey. So catalytic leaders do not go ahead to show the way, but instead provide the spark which ignites others to embark on a mutual venture. If practitioners do not believe they have a stake in what happens then it is difficult for them to feel part of any developments and committed to ongoing improvement. To travel with others requires recognition of different strengths and of the importance of *relational interdependence*, so an important aspect of catalytic agency is the ability to value and empower others to be involved. This requires confidence; not necessarily confidence as a personal characteristic but the professional confidence that comes from genuine commitment and self-belief. Creativity is also a feature and is evident in the ability to build on the opportunities which are available rather than trying to bring about sweeping change that could make others feel intimidated or insecure.

An example of catalytic agency in practice is Ellie who, inspired by the creative use of treasure baskets she observed in another setting, gradually introduced a number of open-ended resources to support heuristic play with 3- and

4-year-olds in her pre-school group. The children's evident interest and involvement impressed both her room supervisor and the manager who became very enthusiastic about the new approach. Ellie also successfully involved parents, helping them to recognize the learning that was taking place and they began to contribute items from home such as leaking hosepipes and old clocks to take apart. Thus from one small initial step Ellie brought about a change which ultimately affected the planning, curriculum, routines, resources and partnership with parents and continues to impact on the way the entire setting works. She recognized the value of a gentle approach and said 'small changes can have a big impact on views and ideas and it is often . . . more effective to instigate change in this manner.'

This example demonstrates that catalytic agency does not need to be dramatic to make a difference and indeed it is more likely to be effective when practitioners avoid the dramatic to concentrate on modest and achievable outcomes. Sensitivity and a measure of humility are therefore essential components of catalytic agency – the ability to resist 'ownership' of ideas and remember that good practice should not be about personal recognition but the ability to make a difference. Being proprietorial and not letting others in has no part in leadership and shows a lack of confidence in needing to claim the glory. A catalyst sets off a process; sometimes this may involve sowing an idea so that others may pick it up and develop it themselves, not as a matter of being underhand and fooling others but of ensuring that everyone has a personal stake in identifying what could be better and taking responsibility for making this happen. Catalytic leadership enables others to shape a germ of an idea into something new, possibly sparking others' ideas in different directions. They set things off, not necessarily forming the idea or solution themselves but providing the fertile ground which enables others to do something with or about it – in this way ownership becomes irrelevant. This concern to involve and empower other practitioners stems from recognition of *relational interdependence* and is a very different approach to the traditional view of leadership taking a position in the forefront. Catalytic agency reflects the two dimensions of inner and diffused action and so may work on an individual basis or else in a group, collective or organizational form as a catalytic organization. The leadership profiles in Chapters 4 and 7 explore catalytic agency in practice.

Reflective integrity

The stance adopted in the paradigm of *leadership within* is that reflection is an integral part of the leadership process and needs to operate both individually and organizationally. Our contention is that leadership without reflection is not true leadership, as without reflection behaviours, actions, events and consequences go unexamined and the process becomes one of exertion of power. Even at its most benign, the exertion of power or influence without reflection is likely to produce misguided leadership. Such leadership is liable to be unaware of what is really happening in the organization, within teams, or in relationships with other organizations, professionals and service users. These situations are characterized by problems arriving unexpectedly because issues are not recognized or remain unresolved to fester, and expected outcomes are not met. Reflection provides the mechanism which prompts learning and understanding. It produces revised or new thinking and encourages action to incorporate this into behaviours and practice.

Integrity means enacting values in practice and at the personal level requires self-awareness to know what matters to us and motivates us. In the context of the organization it requires synergy between mission, vision, policy and practice. Individual and organizational integrity come together in the leadership process and need to have some degree of alignment to create shared purpose. This requires openness to difference, acknowledging that different belief systems and ways of interpreting values can be accommodated and co-exist within common value boundaries and it therefore has much in common with *relational interdependence*. Goleman *et al.* (2002) suggest that integrity can be reduced to a single question which asks if what you are doing is in keeping with your own values. In the paradigm of *leadership within* we go beyond this, not only to ask this question of both the individual and the collective organization but also to demand deeper reflection which examines values relative to the situation in the complex operational context of practice, paying regard to the viewpoint of others. This process is undertaken through the medium of *reflective integrity*.

The feature of reflective integrity which characterizes this paradigm emphasizes the need for reflection to go beyond the surface to check assumptions behind actions, behaviour and relationships, to examine their influence and to be prepared to review underlying tacit knowledge which shapes day-to-day behaviour. This tacit knowledge, revealed through our everyday actions, instinctive responses and interactions, is what Schön (1991) termed 'knowing in action', which is expertise and accumulated knowledge applied automatically in familiar or new situations. While it is based on expertise built on experience, it nevertheless needs examination to check its continuing reliability and whether there is any disparity developing between our actions and our beliefs and values. Reflective integrity aids this process by challenging review of underlying, often unspoken, beliefs and values to enable reasoned discrimination in complex situations while remaining true to ourselves. This is akin to what Argyris and Schön (1996) term double-loop learning, which feeds reflection back to review not only the consequences of action but the strategies and values on which it was based. By using the term reflective integrity we intend to emphasize not only the value base of such reflection but also its potential application as a social competence.

Reflective integrity requires a willingness to challenge and be challenged in the process of reflective review, yet includes a need for reconciliation so that disparities are addressed with honest appraisal without causing a crisis of conscience or confidence. By way of contrast, integrity in reflection is important to prevent complacency where review becomes simple reaffirmation of actions and beliefs without serious scrutiny. This is not the traditional language of leadership and requires a certain bravery to examine and recognize positives and negatives, knowns and unknowns, causes and effects (including those which are unexpected).This can lead to finding areas where strengthening or adapting leadership behaviour and processes may make a positive difference and being willing to try them out. In reflective integrity, leadership is less about power and knowledge and more about accepting that we might not know. It does not, however, leave a sense of powerlessness or inadequacy because it returns to the fundamental reference point of underlying purpose, mission and values to provide orientating criteria for moving forward. It requires a level of confidence and support to challenge, reconcile and learn from experience and reflection. One aspect of much-needed support is the space and time for reflection alone and to share in reflective integrity with others, recognizing our *relational interdependence*. It also requires the ability to give and receive feedback in constructive dialogue with a common understanding about purpose which goes beyond the personal. This is a shared sense of mission and understanding which values the potential of each individual to contribute in a way that also enables them to be true to themselves. The benefit to the individual and the organization is that reflective integrity supports working on principles and towards long-term goals, providing satisfaction and motivation to continue striving and overcoming obstacles. Through the leadership process, reflective integrity enables thoughtful action with examined conviction.

While Schön (1991) identified three temporal levels of reflection ('knowing in action' (immediate, unconscious); 'reflection in action' (thinking in a new way, consciously, in a situation); 'reflection on action' (review after an event)), reflective integrity provides an orientating perspective as a tool to employ regardless of time and place. It applies as much to behaviours and approaches as to the problem or situation. Reflective integrity is explored in Chapters 5 and 8.

Relational interdependence

The paradigm of *leadership within* adopts the view that everyone is capable of contributing towards leadership and that active involvement in the process of leadership should not reside in one or two high-status individuals alone. This makes *relational interdependence* a key component.

Relationships are clearly a significant aspect of education and, in particular, the early years where the affective element of interaction with young children and the development of respectful, sensitive and trusting relationships with their parents and carers is seen as fundamental. In addition, the moral valuing of colleagues and other practitioners brings a further dimension to the professional relationships that are indispensable to leadership. However, *relational interdependence* goes beyond straightforward notions of relationships *per se* and may perhaps best be summed up as the connectivity in our actions and interactions – the recognition that, in order to be effective, we need each other.

Traditional paradigms of leadership are built on notions of power wherein certain individuals take control and decide what should be done. Such a model takes account of relationships in terms of a necessary ingredient for a leader to persuade others to follow their direction. Leadership from within does not rest on invested power and so the relational aspect is richer and more complex. While it is important to acknowledge that hierarchies and power may still exist, by recognizing the complementarity of other colleagues nobody should be precluded from taking on a leadership role. Relational interdependence therefore becomes an important strength of both the group and the individual and participation is built on the sharing of power and respect for others. It can operate not only inside the organization but also in relations with other groups in the community.

Relational interdependence does not simply happen even within groups of colleagues who have worked well together over a considerable period of time. It needs to be encouraged and nurtured. This means cultivating a 'valuing culture' (Canning 2009: 26) which actively welcomes co-dependency as a positive attribute. Such a culture enables us to recognize the possibilities that others offer without feeling that our own role is threatened or undermined in any way by their competence. Equally it recognizes that the ability to make an active and important contribution is unconnected to authority if each person's potential is fostered and they are encouraged to have a meaningful input. Canning points out how the 'development of self-concept and self-image seems to be low on the priority list for individuals and leaders' (2009: 33) although it is crucial to developing and sustaining a nurturing and productive work context. Recognition of relational interdependence moves the emphasis of leadership from directing others towards acknowledging their matching potential and thus enhances their self-image as contributors to an inclusive community. In this way everyone may be actively involved and the relational ethos among colleagues follows that adopted with children – the crucial principle being that of starting from the individual and their strengths rather than working with a deficit model that sees only incompleteness. Such complementary and shared activity emphasizes the mutuality of relational interdependence.

Relational interdependence emerges from a culture which encourages professional dialogue and therefore supports *reflective integrity*. The exploration and discussion of values is key to developing a professional ethos to underpin recognition and valuing of others' contributions. While it is important to be able to debate and examine ideas and professional principles it must also be recognized that this is more effective when it is viewed as a *process* which sustains a flourishing learning community (Wenger 1998) rather than a way of seeking consensus as an end product. Too much emphasis on agreement and sameness can 'potentially dilute, marginalize or push differences underground' (Murray 2009: 21) rather than encouraging healthy professional debate.

The idea of relational interdependence can be appreciated by considering the movement of interconnected cogs; this analogy also demonstrates the strong connection with *catalytic agency* whereby one cog can set the whole integrated system in motion. Successful networks can be built when relational interdependence is seen as a strength to be valued and power sharing is deliberately encouraged; where work to complement the strengths and diversity of others is conceived as an ongoing task rather than a finished end product. Relational interdependence is explored further in Chapters 6 and 9.

Leadership profiles

The second part of this book explores how the paradigm we propose actually works within the context of early years practice. This is done through the format of leadership profiles which are used to illustrate the different features of *leadership within*. A shared paradigm is one of the contextual elements that Nivala (2002) identifies as crucial to the functioning of leadership and we hope that exploration of this in relation to practitioners' daily lived practice can support shared discussion and debate. The profiles consider a wide range of practice and provision within the maintained, private and voluntary sectors. Most, but not all, of the practitioners investigated in Part II are EYPs. The selection of practitioners, however, was made for pragmatic reasons as EYPS is currently the official model for pedagogic leadership in England and both authors have been involved in ongoing research with EYPs. We do not intend to suggest that this is the only way in which leadership might be practised. At the present time public debate about funding for children's services seems likely to affect the future shape of provision in the sector. Although this could mean that EYPS may not always exist in its current form, the need for able, flexible, graduate leaders in the early years will continue to be essential.

Reframing leadership

In Chapter 2, we argued the need for a paradigm shift with which to reconceptualize leadership in the early years (Henderson-Kelly and Pamphilon 2000; Ebbeck and Waniganayake 2003). We recommended that leadership should be seen as quite distinct from management and that it can arise from anywhere within an organization. This chapter puts forward and develops our proposed paradigm of *leadership within*. We suggest that *leadership within* operates on both an inner and a diffused level and that it embraces three identifying features, namely catalytic agency, reflective integrity and relational interdependence. These features can be used to reframe notions of leadership, to examine and debate experiences and to determine future action on an individual as well as a team basis.

The model of *leadership within* moves concepts of leadership not only beyond the traits and characteristics of leaders but also beyond the shared activities and functions as envisaged in ideas of distributed leadership. Spillane suggests that a distributed perspective 'puts leadership practice centre stage' (2006: 25) and, for this reason, it has been put forward as a potentially useful perspective for the early childhood sector (Ebbeck and Waniganayake 2003; Siraj-Blatchford and Manni 2007). Aubrey (2011) appreciates that distributed leadership combines leadership with the characteristics of a learning community and therefore seems particularly pertinent to early childhood settings but recognizes that there are limitations to the model. We concur with her reservation and suggest that distributed leadership offers too narrow a model to align satisfactorily with early years values. We want to shift the focus from activity, tasks and practice which are distributed among others to leadership as a process. In this way there is no need to identify specific tasks of leadership because *leadership within* is a process that can embrace any activity. This process is neither dependent on a positional head nor on fulfilling distributed roles. It can arise from anywhere within an organization and be diffused beyond the individual to 'raise self-awareness and drive, thereby encouraging self-leadership within a community of responsibility' (Murray 2009: 23). The three features of catalytic agency, reflective integrity and relational interdependence all contribute to the process of leadership but can also be envisaged as processes themselves.

The second part of this book is empirically informed and uses research extracts and work conducted across the early years sector to illustrate the paradigm of *leadership within*. A range of different practitioners and aspects of practice are proffered in these leadership profiles to enable us to examine and highlight the process of leadership and make conceptual and empirical links between our theoretical standpoint and practice in the field. The variety of situations examined illustrate how, regardless of whether one considers the curriculum, safeguarding children, partnership with parents or any other aspect of ECEC, it is the processes that shape leadership.

Further reading

McDowall Clark, R. and Baylis, S. (2011) 'Go softly . . .': the reality of 'leading practice' in early years settings, in M. Reed and N. Canning (eds) *Quality Improvement and Change in the Early Years*. London: Sage Publications.
This chapter explores leadership from the perspective of EYPs in practice to consider how catalytic agency is exercised by those with no formal position of authority.

PART II
Leadership profiles

4 Believing you can make a difference: inner catalytic agency

Catalytic agency is founded on a deep commitment to a professional mission which sustains a self-leading approach. It is a process of bringing about change by causing a constructive reaction personally or collectively, within oneself or with others. It builds upon personal recognition that each individual has the ability to make a difference to pedagogical practice thus contributing to children's well-being and learning. Improving children's well-being and learning is the central purpose for both leadership and professional practice in ECEC, so everyone can potentially exercise leadership in contributing to that purpose, regardless of the position held in the organization. This inclusive and participative concept of leadership is fundamental to *leadership within*.

Passionate care

The desire to promote and protect children's well-being and learning is commonly expressed in education circles as 'passion' (Moyles 2001; Day 2004). In discussions with parents, teachers and learners in the school context, Kaser and Halbert (2009) found 'passion' close to or at the top of the list of what makes effective leadership. Marquardt (2000: 3) argues that '[t]rue leadership emerges from those whose prime motivation is a desire to help others' and this desire has been found to be extensively present in those who enter the care and education professions (Moyles 2001; Rodd 2006; Osgood 2010). Taggart (2011: 85) argues that the ECEC profession should be more robust in using the vocabulary of care because it is 'a sustainable element of professional work'. The ethic of care involves the maintenance of caring relationships and guides professional action, placing the interests of children at the forefront of decision-making. Leadership in ECEC, therefore, should embody and advocate caring as a social principle. Passionate commitment to the mission or moral purpose of ECEC, combined with a strong ethic of care, characterizes ECEC professionalism, producing an emotional drive which could be termed *passionate care*, as depicted in Figure 4.1.

Figure 4.1 Passionate care

Passionate care is an active state of professionalism where the desire to make a positive difference to the lives of young children and their families is coupled with belief that improvements can be made. The commitment to moral purpose combined with the responsibility inherent in the ethic of care means that passionate care can generate an emotional drive which fuels catalytic agency. This is not a vain belief in one's own ability or a single-minded quest but an individual or collective professional determination to contribute positively to the social purpose of ECEC. Passionate care encourages ECEC professionals to persevere in the face of challenges and take action to change practice. This reflects a humanistic and phenomenological perspective emphasizing the agentive and subjective power of individuals to construct reality (Rogers 1983) in contrast to structural determinism, which sees organizations as controlling and containing through invested power and position (Spillane *et al.* 2004). Belief in the individual ability to make a difference enables broad participation in and exercise of leadership, unlike traditional views which encourage leadership dependency on the few at the top of the hierarchy.

Inner catalytic agency draws on passionate care to produce a humble confidence that every individual has the capacity and capability to effect change which can have a positive impact, no matter how small. This might be a change in their individual practice or a contribution to changing practice with others. In both cases, self-belief and professional confidence are integral to the process yet these aspects are frequently underplayed in the ECEC sector. Both Moyles (2001) and Osgood (2010) stress the need for professional confidence because 'it is difficult to fight for what one believes in if one has a relatively fragile self-concept and self-confidence' (Moyles 2001: 87) and this can be disempowering and debilitating. Inner catalytic agency can provide the momentum to gain professional confidence and overcome negative emotions in order to work for a higher purpose. Murray (in press) found this to be the case for a group of undergraduate candidates on a pilot programme leading to Early Years Professional Status who were acutely aware of their relative lack of experience in comparison with some of the practitioners in the settings where they were expected to model and lead practice. The candidates were motivated by passionate care which spurred them to identify how they could gain professional confidence and work to gain the respect and acceptance of their fellow practitioners. This meant adopting strategies to build relationships and trust and find ways of working *'to make things better from the middle'* which would enable them to demonstrate their capability (Murray in press). The candidates felt that the way to make an impact was to demonstrate congruence between their beliefs and behaviour in practice. These ways of working were not reliant on power or authority, as they had none as student practitioners, but drew on an internal drive akin to 'self-leadership' (Gill 2006: 11) which provides the motivation derived from doing something worthwhile. The strength of passionate care seems to be central to catalytic agency, sustaining perseverance to overcome obstacles. These EYP candidates expected challenge and prepared themselves for it, drawing on self-resource and determination not to be fearful of trying different strategies. They knew that by taking responsibility and initiative and being prepared to take risks, they would gain the professional confidence they needed. They saw success as lying in their own hands. These candidates demonstrated catalytic agency born of passionate care which enabled them to be self-leading in realizing their professional goals. They aspired to EYPS as a professional identity 'guided by a common morality' (Murray in press). This self-leading approach is integral to catalytic agency, moving aspiration into action.

Passionate care also generates constructive discontent as an emotional driver to catalytic agency. Constructive discontent will not accept the status quo but urges action to find ways of making things better, as Tom demonstrates in Chapter 5 when he says 'What personally drives me is when I feel something doesn't sit right and I know I have to do something about it.' We argue that passionate care is the core of ECEC professionalism, yet it remains relatively unacknowledged as a powerful resource for catalytic agency and inner leadership.

The place of reflection

Catalytic agency often stems from the process of reflective integrity (Chapters 5 and 8), examining practices and problems against values, beliefs and aspirations, looking for possible ways forward and then taking responsibility for actively putting espoused theory into practice. In this way, catalytic agency encourages proactive involvement in the leadership process. The following extracts from an interview with Sarah, a voluntary pre-school leader and EYP, show how the process of reflection led to confident self-belief in her professional purpose and prompted catalytic agency.

On a visit to Reggio Emilia, Italy, Sarah experienced a cycle of challenging emotions and reflections when faced with ways of working which differed from what she considered current practice in her own country. In this case, the reflective process gave impetus and confidence to challenge respectfully and examine her ideals and values against practice. Sarah's underlying desire to learn supports openness to change. Inner catalytic agency takes this process further, stimulating action to improve self and influence others.

> When we went to Reggio, I went on a big cycle of a journey. I felt I was in pre-school Disneyland – the pre-school centre of the world. It was almost overwhelming because they were so good, the environment was so wonderful. Everything seemed to be so much more idealistic, the way I wanted it to be here. So I was in awe of everything and it made me a bit down because it made me think in practice we could never replicate that.

For Sarah, the initial impression of practice on this visit produced awe and perhaps an enviable desire to work in the same way. This quickly led to a feeling of sadness, seeing it as unachievable and feeling unable to do something similar in her home environment. She did not, however, allow her awe to overwhelm her for long.

> And then after a couple of days I started to look a bit critically, perhaps as a defence – thinking, well I'm not that bad! I started to think, why don't they ever go outside or have sand and water? They have sinks but they don't have water trays. The ratio in the baby room was 1:7 and I thought 'Gosh, that's quite high.' They call everyone teacher so I was not sure what sort of training they had. They seemed to just take people on and train them. So I became quite critical about those sorts of things.

This demonstrates that initial responses to new and different practice can be quite negative and produce uncertainties and defensiveness concerning one's own practice. There is a danger of leaving it there and falling at the first hurdle of learning when lack of professional confidence inhibits openness to new ideas. Where the underlying desire to improve practice for children's learning overrides this uncertainty it encourages looking more deeply. So Sarah's next response was to take a critical perspective comparing this provision with aspects she valued in practice. Again, however, this was not left at the level of criticism of what was observed or a defensive review of her practice; instead the reflective cycle continued:

> And then I changed again and started to respect what they had done and to see that it was different from what we had and that we had different priorities. I took from it, I suppose a bit heartening, that although we have the curriculum we can still be fluid and use it to document what the children are doing rather than teach specific aspects of it.

Here Sarah is acknowledging that principles of good practice can be achieved in different ways to suit different circumstances and contexts. Her negative feelings have given way to realization that this is not impossible but needs interpretation and creative thinking to achieve the desired purpose. This is a more self-empowering perspective as it creates the capacity for learning from the experience rather than being deflated by it or prevented from seeing possibilities. Debilitating emotions of defensiveness and lack of self-belief can be toxic for leadership as they hinder the catalytic process which spurs action. Psychologists, such as Gallwey (2002) and Dweck (2002), remind us of the consequent loss to individuals and society from unrealized human potential due to negative or self-defeating thinking and behaviour. These inner obstacles inhibit new ways of thinking and being but the power of reflective integrity and passionate care provide the purposeful belief necessary to overcome them. Then the force of catalytic agency takes a step towards making a change. Sarah shows how she gained 'heart' from the confidence the Reggio practitioners had in themselves and their pedagogy and this spurred her on beyond those initially negative feelings and doubts to look for possibilities and ways to make what she values happen. She sees there is flexibility in her home system to work in a way which will further the pedagogical principles she holds dear and can see in operation in Reggio and this provides impetus and resolution.

> So I started again to appreciate what they had done and did not try to replicate it here but to learn from the confidence they had to believe in themselves and believe in the children and believe that they would come up with their own things and their own interests.

At the end of this reflective cycle, Sarah has come to a point where she can appreciate the good qualities in what she is observing and look to learn from it, identifying what can support her mission. She has identified the need for professional confidence and self-belief aligned to pedagogical mission to effect this change. There is a sense of needing courage to do this and anticipation that it will not necessarily be easy.

Believing you can make a difference

Sarah went through a process of reflective integrity (reflection aligned to examination of beliefs and values), enabling critical challenge with reference to what she holds dear in her mission and practice. This led to respect for a form of practice in a different context from her own and a desire to learn in order to bring about change in her home practice and situation. She recognized that self-belief in the ability to make a difference and professional confidence in the overall purpose and aims are necessary to bring about change. Professional confidence has been identified as a key factor in research related to professionalism and leadership in the ECEC sector (Moyles 2001; Rodd 2006; Osgood 2010; Murray in press) and it needs to be nurtured for catalytic agency to take effect. The small rewards of daily practice help to sustain self-belief, as Sarah comments:

> You have to believe you can make a difference, otherwise you can get down some days and think this is too hard and nothing is changing but there is something inside that makes you respond to the children and when you see a response back it is so rewarding you want to keep doing it. Yes, it does sustain me because you know there will be times when it will get better.

The intrinsic reward and pleasure from working with young children has been well documented as a motivational effect for ECEC professionals (Moyles 2001; Osgood 2010; Murray in press). Yet the ethic of care has also been seen as a paradox, making practitioners vulnerable to exploitation because the appeal to selfless service can be used unscrupulously (Osgood 2010; Taggart 2011). This concern reinforces a view of early years as lacking status and professional strength without the ability to defend its position and purpose, which could encourage defeatism. Alternatively, the ethic of care could be used more positively to show fundamental professional resolve in common purpose. If practitioners are encouraged to feel that putting children first is a weakness it undermines the passionate care at the very heart of their professional ethic. It also reduces confidence and self-belief, which reduces agency. So we would argue that passionate care for furthering the interests of young children supports professional confidence, providing motivation, determination and responsibility to act. It is the driver for catalytic agency.

Sarah took responsibility to turn her experience of Reggio into an active response on her return.

> Then I looked at the environment completely differently [she continues to describe some physical changes made to the learning environment] and started to look at being creative rather than just accepting what I had, in a very small way trying to change things.

In this case, the trip to Reggio provided the catalyst for reflective integrity, which prompted recognition of the need for agency to take action to change practice. The renewal of self-belief and confidence supported the process of catalytic agency, drawing on constructive discontent not to accept the way things are but to do something about it. This doesn't necessarily involve wholesale or dramatic change – it is often more effective in small incremental steps (McDowall Clark and Baylis 2011).

Sustaining impetus

The desire to continue to seek ways to improve is fundamental to catalytic agency. It works with passionate care and constructive discontent to see possibilities and take opportunities to move the vision forward, persisting and overcoming obstacles. Catalytic agency is about having a vision and taking responsibility for actively working towards it.

> I suppose I went looking for somebody else doing it a different way. Looking for hope really, having read a lot about it. Hope that there was something else other than this [alluding to familiar practice in this country] which seems to be quite prescriptive and I have struggled coming back.

In going to Reggio, Sarah was purposely seeking inspiration, using the opportunity to observe another way of working. On her return, however, she experienced feelings of despondency when she was faced with the conflict between her values and ideals and the reality of practice and official expectations.

> We had to do this big presentation on how creative everything was in Reggio and we had gone through the poem 'The 100 languages of children'. I talked about how adults teach children to think without their bodies, disconnecting bodies and minds, hands and head when they do letters and sounds in this country. It just seems so removed from finding a snail, making a park for the snail and learning the way the child wants to learn. I still struggle with reconciling those two things.

Catalytic agency is fuelled by the desire to make things better for children as the core purpose of early years work and the sense of passion about children's learning is apparent in this extract. It gives the impetus to influence others working for a common mission, appealing to root pedagogical principles.

> We were paid to go by the council, as the first EYPs, and they wanted us to come back and say this [the creativity of Reggio approach]. We did a presentation and everyone was enthusiastic then straight away they had this letters and sounds specialist teaching us how to clap out the syllables. I just looked around and thought, 'Am I the only person who feels that this is exactly what they were *not* saying?' Yet still letters and sounds are pushed wherever we go and the Reggio bit has just been dropped by the wayside, 'Oh well that's a nice experience. . .and now go back to reality!'

Sarah's sense of outrage and unacceptability of this is palpable and demonstrates the motivating power of constructive discontent which does not countenance living with unacceptable compromise of principles. Sarah feels she cannot just let go of her pedagogical beliefs but recognizes that promoting them is not always easy.

> I really struggle and push others to look at the whole picture: to see what they are learning is not about skills but dispositions and attitudes. This is something I have always been passionate about. I've wanted to teach children to think rather than how to write their name with dots and those kinds of things and that is still my vision.

Working with a vision is acknowledged to be a struggle. It requires perseverance and resolution. It needs deliberate, constructive and sustained action without which it would remain at discontent and become disabling. This is where the underlying passionate care for young children and belief in the ability to make a difference gives confidence and hope to sustain catalytic agency.

Encouraging others

In the dimension of inner leadership, catalytic agency needs a certain autonomous ability to act and be self-regulating and self-leading to enable fulfilment of purpose. It also entails a sense of responsibility for taking it further within one's own sphere of influence in professional practice. The ability to influence practice is not confined to those in positions of authority and is part of professional practice; however, in this case the practitioner, Sarah, considered that her role as an EYP and pre-school leader gave additional responsibilities – those of sharing knowledge and supporting the learning of colleagues.

> You have to create the conditions with the team, so that they feel important and valued and that will help them to believe in themselves, and when you do suggest change or introduce small things, they will go with you on that. They will trust you and feel part of the team.

Encouraging self-belief and developing professional confidence are important for generating engagement in the process of professional practice development. Sarah saw her leadership responsibility as engendering trust through support and respect and building confidence in the team to contribute and participate. Kaser and Halbert (2009) see relational trust as essential in creating positive cultures. They argue that where moral purpose is strong among the parents and staff there is a feeling of obligation to work together for the benefit of the children and relational trust reinforces this. Where trust is high, there is more likelihood of ethical practices and behaviour conducive to collaboration.

> Most educators intuitively understand that they are operating in a community where social capital and the trust it brings to the learning enterprise are critical . . . Relational trust is fundamental to strong learning cultures and has a positive impact on learning outcomes.
>
> (Kaser and Halbert 2009: 47)

While Kaser and Halbert lay the responsibility for developing trust squarely at the door of the nominated leader, we suggest there is a more reciprocal dimension. Recognition of the need to foster trusting and respectful relationships is important for every practitioner and is achieved through attending to one's everyday interactions with this in mind. Developing mutual trust is part of relational interdependence (see Chapters 6 and 9). This strengthens the potential for inner catalytic agency to have a knock-on effect, provoking a constructive reaction to individual agency by colleagues, parents and children. Developing trust is part of every practitioner's role and a principal way in which they participate in the process of *leadership within*; it is also a key requirement of the formal leader.

For Sarah, the process of building leadership trust is taken slowly and is fostered by working in a consultative and inclusive manner, valuing different ideas and examining them collectively against pedagogical principles.

> At staff meetings we talk about what the children are learning and how we can plan; for example, someone might say, 'Shall we get the egg boxes out and make daffodils?' and then I might say, 'What about getting some daffodils and start by getting the children to smell them and draw or paint them, if that's what they want to do?' and then someone else will say, 'That's a good idea as it gives the children choice and it is more open-ended.'

This is a conscious approach to encourage different ways of thinking, gaining momentum towards collective change by encouraging, supporting and involving others. Catalytic agency is not an automatic process but requires attention to relationships and building ways of working which nurture the drive and confidence in others to make things better.

> When we do the planning I will ask, 'How did it go?' and they say, 'Oh they were great, so and so did this or we need a lot more practice at this.' When you have those dialogues it keeps other people fresh and you can ask them, 'What do you think we could do next?' I think it is just keeping everybody involved and feeling they are important and that they are part of how the children are learning as well.

Catalytic agency prompts thinking about possible ways of working and how each person can participate and contribute towards the common goal by keeping the overall purpose in mind. This involves supporting each other to move away from self-restricting thinking and behaviour, releasing talents through encouragement and genuine respect. Appreciation of relational inter-dependency encourages working deliberately and collectively to build a positive, enriching and ambitious culture in which everyone has a valued part to play. Sarah is nurturing the leadership components which enable collective growth by emphasizing that everyone is important and part of the process, making this a common quest and bolstering self-belief. Dialogue helps to maintain the relationships and reinforces the collective endeavour.

Sarah sees her leadership as modelling and gentle influence, using the support and trust of like-minded members of staff to help demonstrate how their shared purpose and pedagogical values can be put into practice.

> I suppose I model a lot and influence and I think you look for the ones in your team who do have the same philosophy and you can take some comfort from talking to them and getting excited with them about the things you are doing and when you have staff meetings you hope they will come alongside. I'd rather convince than be confrontational. There is no point in making people do it because they won't if they don't believe in it.

The significance of common values and pedagogical beliefs at the heart of professional practice is tacitly understood and can be appealed to as a rallying point to encourage others to promote, sustain and engage in change.

> You have to have those values, this professional love for children. We remind everybody what the values are, as it is easy for practitioners who have been in early years for a long time to fall back on habits. We have to remind ourselves that we are here for the children and it is not about us. Once you understand that, you understand that we don't tidy away at half past ten and then sit down for half an hour register or tidy up and keep everyone waiting for snacks to be brought to them. We are about getting the children to peel the carrots, spread their own butter, to come and have something to eat if they want to. Tidy up was a routine that, for a long time, staff couldn't see why it had to change. So you keep reminding them why it is important, why we made this change because we believe that children need long stretches of time when they can get into a state of flow where learning and development is really happening.

Catalytic agency requires maintenance to keep the reasons for change and the benefits uppermost in your own thinking and in other people's minds. This can be draining but the small successes and recognition of the ability to make a difference to children help to sustain personal drive.

> The joys and successes keep you going. You try to model in the way you work with children, like this morning we found caterpillars and made a house for them. Now we can't see them because they are covered in the grass and I explained that it was camouflage. Helping the children to collect those little leaves and what the caterpillars needed in order to live was one of those rewarding moments. The children put water in and put a lid on. They respond so much to that interest that you want to do the same with adults as well – to show an interest in them and lead in the same way.

Here, Sarah is making connections between pedagogy, andragogy and leadership, seeing the potential for interrelating principles of child and adult learning with leadership. Co-construction is a central principle of early years pedagogy which has been effectively translated into pedagogical leadership in the form of learning communities or communities of practice. Strong teams make time to debate and discuss their practice, articulating and sharing pedagogical knowledge and learning (Whelan 2006). In order to sustain effective change and growth, early years organizations need to develop a learning culture, breaking down inhibiting barriers and negative emotions which stunt growth. Developing genuine relationships is fundamental to this, where there is concern and respect for each individual combined with a belief in their capability. Sarah wants to translate her pedagogical framework to the leadership process, in the way she works with others. She likens this to driving the bus, taking people with you, rather than command and control. She hopes to provide the stimulus or catalyst to prompt involvement and actively creates an ethos of sharing, listening and openness to learning and ideas.

> When I came back from Reggio I did buy quite a few books to share what it was like and I suppose I kind of inspired them a bit, saying things like 'Just imagine there is no curriculum! The children do all these things, look how they set it out' because I knew they would respond to some pictures which look just wonderful. So I just laid them on the table and let them look through and said 'Do you think there is anything that we could do that we could bring a little bit of this back to our setting?' You have to push but you have to walk slowly otherwise you lose them.

Conclusion

This interview extract has shown aspects of catalytic agency in the individual process of one's person's practice. We offer this as an investigation of purposeful activity as it occurs in practice. Spillane *et al.* (2004: 9) argue that the practice situation should be the unit of leadership study because it demonstrates the 'mutuality of the individual and the environment', forming 'an interactive web of actors, artefacts and situation'. It provides the opportunity to understand leadership processes better by examining where and how they take place, socially with other people. We differ, however, in that Spillane *et al.* (2004) consider leadership activity takes place through tasks, whereas we are examining the purposes and processes that are taking place. The sense of responsibility to work with, support and engage others in effecting change is part of Sarah's personal professional practice, heightened by her interpretation of her designated role as the pre-school leader, rather than any particular tasks associated with that role. Her sense of responsibility is more integral to her core professionalism underpinned by passionate care to adopt pedagogical practices that will benefit children's learning and well-being. This provides an emotional drive to sustain working to make things better, releasing catalytic agency in her personal practice and with others. Catalytic agency is a manifestation of self-leadership and characterizes *leadership within*.

Reflective prompts

To summarize:

Catalytic agency

- can arise out of reflection and reflective integrity;
- draws on constructive discontent and determination to improve;
- can overcome negative emotions and attitudes;
- requires and supports professional confidence and self-belief;
- leads to action to change;
- has an impact on self-learning and can trigger change in others;
- builds relational interdependency as part of agency for change.

1 Take two of these points and examine where they occur in the interview extract.
2 Where can you see evidence of this or similar scenarios in your own practice or experience?
3 How can the arguments in this chapter help you to develop greater catalytic agency?

---

5 'Finding it on your way': inner reflective integrity

It is patently apparent that the early years sector is dominated by female staff (Muijs *et al.* 2004; Dunlop 2005; Siraj-Blatchford and Manni 2007) and this has particular implications for male practitioners who at best are considered unusual in their career choice and may even be regarded with suspicion and mistrust (Sargent 2005).

The topic of men in the early years sector has been examined from a range of perspectives (Owen *et al.* 1998; Cameron *et al.* 1999; Cameron 2001; Owen 2003; Rolfe 2005; Cameron 2006), and there exists also a sub-set of debates in connection with the particular issue of women's leadership (Scrivens 2002). It can be tempting to use a feminist slant to explain the prevalence of nurturing styles of leadership (Hall 1996; Whalley 1999; Henderson-Kelly and Pamphilon 2000) in terms of a predominantly female workforce but, as we outlined in Chapter 2, we consider this to be a false correlation and consequently a misleading argument. Instead we would suggest that such nurturing attitudes stem directly from the ethic of care (Gilligan 1989), the 'moral seriousness' of which is central to professionalism (Taggart 2011: 85). Professionalism aligned with care underpins a commitment to fostering relationships which support growth and sustain learning, and although this has traditionally been associated with women it need not, and indeed should not, be seen as primarily a gendered undertaking. What is crucial, though, is the element of reflective integrity which encourages self-awareness and serves as the necessary motivation for operating at a high level of criticality.

Perspectives on gender

Although we argue that gender is not a helpful explanatory framework for examining leadership, it would be foolish to deny that the different embodiment of male practitioners does not bring with it an altered perspective from the norm. Being a man in a female-dominated environment provides an array of issues which open up debates and contribute to what Claire Cameron (2006: 76) has referred to as 'multiple ways of knowing'. An important element of reflective integrity is the consideration of differences in viewpoints, experiences and approaches to make visible that which may previously have been unseen.

Writing in connection with call centres, Deborah Cameron (2008: 5) points out how male applicants 'have to prove that they possess the necessary skills, whereas women are just presumed to possess them'; the same is true of early years settings where women are assumed to be the norm and male workers are positioned as 'other' (Sumsion 2000). Such gendered expectations demonstrate the persistence of mid-twentieth-century functionalist ideas in which complementary gender roles were seen as necessary for the smooth running of society. The function of the male within a consensual model of society was identified by Talcott Parsons as 'instrumental', and he suggested it should be balanced by women's more 'expressive' role (Parsons and Bales 1956). While later feminist critiques challenged such views, creating a context for equal opportunities and greater social justice, perceptions of the early childhood worker as substitute mother remain firmly entrenched both within broader society and in the sector itself. As a result the role is not only strongly gendered but also devalued by assumptions that little or no education is necessary to undertake such work (Moss 2006). If the sector aspires to 'democratic professionalism' (Oberheumer 2005) then reflective integrity is crucial to make visible the attitudes and beliefs which sustain such a limiting maternal discourse (Ailwood 2008).

The inheritance of instrumental and expressive functions is evident in debates about women's leadership which reject traditional male attitudes in favour of collaborative and co-operative approaches. For instance, Cubillo (1999) points out how effective leadership has traditionally been explained by recourse to 'stereotypically androcentric' characteristics relating to power and competition whereas women are more likely to consult and share power within non-hierarchical groups. Henderson-Kelly and Pamphilon (2000) propose that the move to develop new styles of early years leadership is driven by recognition that traditional male values and attributes are not relevant to the sector and Scrivens (2002) advocates that research into women's styles of leading opens up new and more valid ways of working. The importance of maintaining female affective values against the threat of increasingly technocratic and instrumental practices has been argued by Osgood (2006a, 2006b); she does not claim, however, that it is only women who can operate in the affective domain. We propose therefore that it is time to move beyond gendered debates towards a more inclusive paradigm of leadership. Furthermore, we suggest that nurturing, collaborative styles of working in the early years exist, not because those displaying such behaviours are female (there is after all a mathematical likelihood that they will be), but because it is in the nature of the work. Men in early years do the same; it is a feature of the sector and its value base and any attempt to explain it away as a female characteristic both undermines professionalism and marginalizes male practitioners. Nonetheless, the very fact that they are in a minority makes the interface between their gender and leadership worth investigating as men are working in a distinctive position where their daily experiences can offer increased awareness of self and encourage reflection on this. This is not to suggest that men may reflect where women do not, but simply that their often unique position is likely to prompt reflection about themselves as childcare professionals in rather different ways from women who work in a sector for which society considers them eminently suited. This chapter therefore considers the experience of two male practitioners to illustrate how the feature of reflective integrity contributes to the paradigm of *leadership within*.

How significant is gender?

Tom and Daniel entered the field of early childhood from quite different directions; Daniel is in his mid-twenties and studied for a BTEC Diploma before working in private day care whereas Tom, who is in his late thirties, had previously worked in stereotypically male occupations before he became a childminder and then began work in a rural pre-school. At the time of interview both men worked in Children's Centres. Tom, about to move on to a new post of formal leadership, is particularly aware of the effect and significance of his gender in the workplace:

> I'm very conscious with my new job. . .I've always worked with women and been quite grateful. It will be strange to move out of being line-managed purely from my own safeguarding point of view. For instance, in my first year there was a situation with a parent who was quite upset about a man working in the setting. She wasn't comfortable with it at all and made an accusation that her child was being sexually abused. Thankfully, my manager was very supportive and dealt with it very professionally. There were policies and procedures to follow obviously but I was very thankful that I was well looked after. And the parent was perfectly happy to let her child continue in the setting for several years before he moved on so clearly she didn't have any serious misgivings – it was anxiety about a male member of staff. I think establishing the nursery as a place of trust is possibly even more important for men than it is for women. So I've always worked really hard to develop good working relationships and a culture where people can speak their mind – if I was a quieter, more withdrawn person that might be harder of course. So it's not completely equal opportunities – I have to work hard to make sure I don't offend anyone, or that if I do I account for it and

try to address things as soon as they come up. Arguing a point can be difficult sometimes because of my different background: coming from construction and before that a military background I've had to learn to speak quite differently. I've learned to use phrases such as 'It seems like. . .', 'I've noticed that. . .', 'Could you maybe help me with. . .?' I think of it as post-modernistic language; it doesn't speak from absolutes but instead of saying things outright uses phrases like 'seeming to' and 'it might be'. I think men often use absolutes – for instance I would say, 'It is like this' – so for me it's been a matter of moving away from such a definite point of view. In female-dominated environments male language can sometimes appear aggressive, or else be misinterpreted as arrogant.

Here we can see reflective integrity at play in Tom's awareness of the difficulty of negotiating his role within a social environment that may regard him with distrust and cultural unease (Owen 2003; Sargent 2005). He recognizes that the parent's mistrust stems from discomfort when her own assumptions and prejudices are confronted by the presence of a male worker and does not represent personal criticism of himself as a practitioner; this enables him to deal with it in a professional and non-judgemental manner. Furthermore, reflecting on such a reaction has led Tom to think more deeply about 'establishing the nursery as a place of trust' and the need to foster appropriate working relationships and develop a culture where people can speak openly and share concerns. Tom's self-awareness of himself as the lone male worker extends to his consideration of the language which he uses and awareness that male ways of speaking could be (mis)interpreted by female colleagues as abrupt, arrogant or even aggressive. As a result he has learned to modify the way he expresses himself to 'fit' the surrounding culture. This analytical self-questioning and attentiveness to the construction of his professional identity demonstrates a high level of critical self-awareness and reflective integrity as he checks that he is being true to his values and that they remain valid in the way he operates.

In contrast to Tom's experience, Daniel sees little difference between his role and that of female colleagues:

Daniel: I don't know if it has affected my role. When I worked at [my previous nursery] I became immersed into the team right away – I never felt any different. I think the only time I ever felt different was when someone actually mentioned how nice it was to have a male member of staff – and funnily enough that actually became a selling point for the nursery!

Interviewer: I think that lots of nurseries want male staff with little idea why beyond the fact that it offers a different role model.

Daniel: It did become a little bit like that but I didn't actually mind because it's nice to be appreciated in a role that isn't particularly 'male'. But I've never really felt any different, I'm just doing the same job as everyone else – it's just that I may come at it from another point of view. For instance, I really enjoy rough and tumble play. I know that lots of female staff I've worked with don't enjoy it or won't get down on the floor with the children, but I really do. I'm constantly having children throwing themselves on me or trying to get me down on the ground for piggy backs, play fighting and things like that that. It's something I've always done because the children really enjoy it – and I enjoy it! It's good for children too because they get lots of physical exercise as well through it. But otherwise I'd say I'm more or less like everyone else, just a man working in that environment.

Although recognizing that he brings a different perspective, Daniel clearly perceives his role, and is perceived by others, as an early years professional rather than as occupying a specifically gendered role. His self-examination of his role also extends to consideration of how he might be viewed by parents and carers. When he began at the Children's Centre Daniel admits:

I was quite. . .not scared, but apprehensive. . .being a male in early years in a predominantly Muslim and Pakistani community. I thought I might get awkward looks or remarks, perhaps the head would say you're going to have to be moved because the parents don't like it. But I've had nothing but praise, nothing but positive feedback from parents and teachers so that's really set my mind at rest.

Value-based reflection and multiple knowledges

Like Tom, working in an atypical occupation has prompted Daniel to reflect on his gender in a way which female practitioners are not required to do in the course of their daily work. Their own gender is seldom an issue for women working in early years because it is part of the taken-for-granted assumptions that underpin practice; for instance, women are expected to act as good role models to children as an aspect of their professionalism rather than of their gender whereas for men the reverse is often true and their influence is seen primarily in terms of their gender rather than generic professionalism. Confusion surrounds the purpose of men in nurseries; although claimed as 'positive' role models this argument is rarely effectively articulated (Sargent 2005). Daniel's former nursery's appreciation of a male worker could be viewed as tokenism unless accompanied by an explicit understanding of what different perspective he might bring by virtue of his gender. Sargent (2005) has identified three versions of male roles within early childhood: a demonstration of traditional masculinity, representing discipline or else depicting different, gentler forms of masculinity that may not be encountered in the home. The rough and tumble play Daniel mentions (and which we will see is also important to Tom) is most easily identified with traditional masculinity but other ways of being male are also evident when he talks about his emotional attachment to the children:

> I think it's why I really enjoy my job – maybe I get a bit too attached but I think that's a good thing, especially for children here who might not have male role models in their lives or don't see them very much – that can be hard for them.

Both Tom and Daniel, by opening up and articulating perspectives which might not arise without their (male) presence, are constructively reviewing and encouraging others to review existing assumptions, attitudes and beliefs. Thus reflective integrity is a crucial aspect of *leadership within* because it paves the way for democratic practices through the encouragement of plurality and diversity, an acceptance of complexity and of multiple knowledges (Urban 2008). Reflection provides the means for new learning and understanding, prompting revised ways of thinking and encouraging better practice; but purposive and constructive criticism must be based on a moral and ethical foundation which demonstrates its integrity through shared beliefs and values.

The value base which underpins Tom's reflective integrity is strongly apparent:

> I do believe in certain values and truths, and we have to recognize other people by acknowledging their values. Sometimes others may steer away from deeper levels of communication in the workplace but it's very important to have a whole team understanding which requires transparency, and you have to gain trust too. But what motivates me is that I understand what play *should* look like.
>
> I want to be cautious because there are two sides to every story and with the example I'm going to give there were others who interpreted the situation differently. But to bring about change from a non-authoritative position does take humility. And that's something I had to work on – it's not something I had naturally!
>
> One setting where I worked it seemed that the boys were running riot. Their need for some kind of physical outlet was recognized so there was a gym mat provided for rough and tumble play. The practitioners didn't engage in this at all – it was at the back of the room for 'boy play' without staff involvement. The staff were deployed around tables with activities

like puzzles and play dough where mainly girls were involved. There was also a home corner with dressing-up clothes and bikes outdoors. So the boys always ended up either rough and tumbling or outside on bikes. I felt a bit uneasy about the provision and raised concerns about how play was facilitated. I think they were happy to have a man sort out 'boy play' as no one seemed to know where to go with it. I noticed it would build up to a point where one child would hurt another – then the game would finish and they'd move off arguing about whose fault it was. So I brought in rules adapted from the behaviour guidelines and we talked about 'kind hands' and that sort of thing. But that was a bit naff really because you can't do rough and tumble without using your hands! It really wasn't working and levels of involvement seriously dwindled. I decided I'd have to model rough and tumble play with kind hands – to some extent against my better judgement because obviously I was much bigger than the children and I wanted them to be able to negotiate among them-selves. But it seemed this needed to be modelled so I played with three or four boys and we had a rule that if a child said 'Enough! I don't like it' you must stop immediately. The second time we did this a parent walked in and complained to the manager. She said that sort of play was reserved for her son's dad and it wasn't educational. Although I made a real attempt to explain my intentions to the parent and why it was important for the children she went to other boys' parents who all agreed they didn't want me 'teaching boys how to fight'. So I was told it was a no-go area and I was to stop all the rough and tumble.

Like Daniel, Tom realized that his female colleagues were reluctant to engage in rough and tumble play and were happy to leave the 'problem' of physically active boys to a male practitioner, thus supporting Sargent's (2005) suggestion of men being valued not only for embodying traditional male stereotypes but also for providing a measure of discipline among unruly boys. Once again, however, a parent expressed concerns and, without clearer commitment to this type of play from his female colleagues, it was temporarily curtailed. Bringing about change is not always straightforward and practitioners need to recognize that they may meet resistance, need to renegotiate and look for opportunities to take a more step-by-step approach. Tom respected the concerns of others but this did not cause him to change his values or the prin-ciples he works from. Throughout, Tom's reflective integrity is apparent in the way he constructively reviewed provision with others, was receptive to ideas and modelled good practice. This approach meant he was eventually successful in modifying distrustful attitudes:

Then one boy had a pirate-themed birthday party and his parents provided foam swords for all the children. The boys instantly began beating each other up with them and the parents were pulling their hair out! So they gave the swords to our setting. The first day, of course, the boys beat each other with the swords – so we moved on to 'kind swords'! The rule was sword-on-sword play never swords on the body. But the boys were still standing around the play mat so I wanted to bring in props for role play and extend the opportunities. We made battle costumes looking in books at knights' armour – lots of opportunities for language development and much richer play opportunities. We had a superhero day – some boys brought in costumes from home, but, of course, not everyone did so I made props with them. There was lots of mark-making involved as the boys made their own signs such as Super Sam – in fact, all areas of the curriculum. But there was a tendency for play to cut across other quieter areas – for instance, if someone was constructing a car then it might get taken over as a pirate ship and inter-fere with other children's activities. So we needed an area for sword play and superhero play where we could say, 'This is the kind of play that happens in this area – and there's a possibility that you might get hurt, but if you do it is accidental because it is very active.'

But it was difficult – it was great when it was great – but the journey was difficult and I had to take a lot of criticism. Even though I tried to encourage other adults to join me on the journey they were very reluc-tant. Eventually I began to be able to mentor colleagues in using hack-saws and a workbench, so for instance we made picture frames and other practitioners were confident the children would be safe. Perhaps because I am a man I could take risks and overcome fears that held other colleagues back – I don't know. I rarely see rich play opportunities for boys in settings I visit. Perhaps it really needs to be led, because it can look scary and many may feel it is not an acceptable risk; it does need to be very, very active play.

Perseverance is a key factor in catalytic agency to support practice over time and meet challenges but reflective integrity moderates the possibility that this could become single-minded determination to push through one's own ideas instead of considering others and understanding why they may differ. So the concern does not go away but is re-evaluated in order to look for different ways to move practice forward that still match underlying principles. The reflection that enabled Tom to consciously examine his own practice and the provision on offer indicates integrity founded in a strong value base and is necessary for action to be intentional and purposive because 'pedagogical leadership can only be actualized within the limits of the leader's pedagogical consciousness' (Nivala 2002: 18). Resilience is important because there may be reluctance or resistance, as was the case in Tom's situation, and this demonstrates the impor-tance of reflective integrity in constructive review and how male (or other alternative) perspectives may open up to question long-held assumptions. Men who work in early years enter a very feminized environment. Despite espoused intentions to encourage anti-sexist (or, more commonly, non-sexist) practices, the fact that most practitioners are female inevitably means the environments they establish reflect their own preconceptions of what is appropriate. It is frequently instinctive for female practitioners to try to step in and prevent boisterous behaviour. Many practitioners view conflict with alarm and may misinterpret it as 'misbehaviour' rather than supporting children in developing effective conflict resolution strategies (Broadhead 2009). These responses to emotional and social development are taken so much for granted that they are rarely questioned. As a result any alternative male position is viewed as 'other' (Sumsion 2000) so that, although men are theoretically welcomed in early years, in practice their particular contribution is rarely articulated; on occasions it may amount to little more than lip-service where settings are happy to accept male practitioners as long as they act in ways deemed appropriate by their female counterparts. These are challenging and uncomfortable issues to confront and so reflective integrity is crucial for examining attitudes and beliefs and prompting constructive debate. In this way, learning and development at a diffused level come about through reflective integrity exercised at the inner level; the two dimensions are linked and complementary.

The gendering of emotional engagement

Tom's situation also raises the issue of appropriate relationships with young children. The need for emotional care and warmth (Elfer *et al.* 2003) is easily identified with women's role as substitute mothers; Moyles (2001: 82), for instance, in her examination of the 'paradox of passion' points out how difficult it is to 'separate out the mother/formal teacher roles' yet recognizes that they must be combined to meet the individual needs of the child. While such a combination is acceptable and expected of female practitioners there are still those who feel uncomfortable about men's intimate relationships with young children (Owen 2003; Sargent 2005). Passion and a strong sense of mission act as the ethical grounds and motivation for working in early years and an emotional connection with the children in their care is seen as integral to their professionalism by early years practitioners (Moyles 2001; Osgood 2010; Murray in press).The ethic of care, however, is frequently used as a gendered concept (Taggart 2011) and men are not expected to have a passion for young children who are not their own. Nonetheless, this is clearly Daniel's motivation in his work:

> You need to have an emotional drive, you can't work with little ones and be a robot – you must have emotion and attachment. I find it so rewarding

to work with children and be part of their learning journey. It makes the job worth doing if you do get emotional over little things you see and little things you do. You have to have the passion to do it and be able to get emotional, to show it's ok to cry, it's ok to be sad and to be angry. These little ones don't necessarily know that to smile means you're happy; they don't know if you cry it *might* mean that you're sad but it might mean you're happy – you can have happy tears too. You have to be there to show them all this. A few weeks ago I had three or four boys come to me crying because a couple of them had fallen over, one of them wasn't feeling well and one just thought he'd cry because everyone else was crying! So I sat them down on a low brick wall and said, 'Right, this will be our crying spot. So let's all have a cry and get it all out.' They started laughing then because although I was making a joke I also wanted to help them feel better, so that was it and we had a big hug and they went off and played.

Although increasingly recognized as a central aspect of professionalism, the 'emotional labour' (Hochschild 1983) of childcare is not something that is taught as part of practitioners' qualifications and professional development. Instead, care is understood as a 'largely adventitious ingredient in the personality of the successful carer' (Taggart 2011: 90). By contrast, men must work to actively counteract and challenge stereotypes of themselves as insensitive and lacking in emotion. It is less expected that men will talk about children in emotional terms but passion is part of the nature of professionalism (Moyles 2001), as Daniel recognizes:

They're still developing so you need to understand and know about different theories. An understanding of Piaget, Bruner and Vygotsky for instance, these are very much embedded in the EYFS and you can see it every day . . . people with no theoretical knowledge have no context for their practice. I've always been really interested in all that and I think my passion for learning has rubbed off on my friends as well because we have long 'intellectual' conversations which is great because they weren't that interested when we started at uni. So I would like to think my drive and passion has perhaps helped them look back on it all and become more reflective in their own practice – and that's happened without me having to really do anything . . . I think it's passion that makes for professionalism, having that passion to be with the children. And it's that passion that drives people to go and do early years degrees and EYPS. The government needs to recognize this is a profession and that it's the passion of the practitioners which will drive professionalism forward and hopefully take it where it should be and where it needs to be.

Making a difference

The enthusiasm with which Daniel talks about his work incorporates both emotional and cognitive responses which are very much entwined, illustrating Moyles's suggestion that 'for practice to reach professional status both head and heart have to meet at the interface of reflection' (2001: 90). In this way, Daniel demonstrates reflective integrity operating not only at a personal level but also diffused among the wider community of his colleagues. The impact of such an approach illustrates leadership from within whereby the influence of practitioners will be far more than might otherwise be expected from their formal role or position. Reflective integrity is the means by which practitioners look beyond the surface of what is happening to examine, review (and if necessary revise) their underlying knowledge so that practice does not become complacent. There must be a willingness to take responsibility and this requires a constant awareness and receptive frame of mind, as Tom describes:

A lot of time I try to put ideas out and see how people react. I think long and hard about my professional beliefs and what I believe and why. That must always be the basis for making statements or any kind of change. You've got to put your stake in the ground and be prepared to say, 'This is the way we should be doing. . .' and take responsibility for making those sorts of statements. But I've learned there's not just one way to bring about change. Previously I used to be very impulsive – I would make 'impulse statements' immediately if something bothered me. Now I think more deeply and try to be more creative in my responses – for instance, just making a passing comment that makes someone think more deeply about what they're doing and why. It's important to find creative ways to bring about change because of the emotional aspect of feeling criticized. The relationships you form with others are fundamental if you're taking on issues that otherwise will be avoided or ignored. I'm not saying you need acknowledgement because you soon learn in early childhood that extrinsic motivation doesn't work! You've got to be intrinsically motivated because there's little reward outside either financially or in terms of professional respect. The reward is in what drives a person and what personally drives me is when I feel that something doesn't sit right and I know I have to do something about it. And in that I think perhaps being a man might make it more difficult, more difficult to talk through things the way women do – when they socialize they will often resolve issues outside the work situation. . .You've got to find different ways of building that dynamic, which can be difficult. Staff meetings get overtaken by the agenda and there's not space enough to explore ideas,

> bouncing things off each other. Only by 'hanging out' can you tackle
> new ideas without it being emotionally charged. So I work hard to create
> hanging out opportunities so we can talk about practice while we're
> working – talking about provision, how it's set up, how to provide a
> richer experience for the children.

This not only exemplifies Tom's reflective integrity but also demonstrates how
it works in parallel with the other facets of *leadership within*. He takes very seriously his potential to impact on practice through catalytic rather than authoritative leadership and recognizes the relational interdependence at the heart of
any change or improvement. Catalytic agency is apparent in the combination
of creativity and humility as well as his acceptance of evolving progress. At the
same time Tom's perspective draws our attention to the difficulty male practitioners may have in negotiating leadership that avoids stereotypically male,
authoritarian views of leadership. The fact that the majority, if not all, of their
workmates are female can make it harder to meet on an equal footing in ways
which women may be oblivious to.

Leadership and gender are both socially constructed concepts (Berger and
Luckman 1966) and this is liberating because it opens the way to re-envisaging,
reinterpreting and reimagining ways of being. Reflective integrity requires willingness to both challenge and be challenged, which stems from a sense of
inner security and a strong sense of direction to enable early years professionals
to remain future-orientated and persist in the face of obstacles. Both Tom and
Daniel recognize this in different ways:

> *Daniel:* Leadership is listening to everyone and sharing ideas, sharing practice;
> it's compromise and showing you're still willing to learn. Even though
> people may feel they already know everything, you don't ever know all
> that there is to know. You may be wrong sometimes so it's not about
> having the perfect answer but about finding it on your way. You need to
> know your limits and be able to say, 'That's all I can do', not be afraid to
> step back, ask for help, support. You have to involve others and that can
> give them a sense of responsibility. So it must be about sharing the
> journey.
>
> *Tom:* You have to be forgiving to yourself because sometimes it doesn't work
> so you can't take a position as an agent of change as 'all-knowledgeable'.
> There are those of course who just want to perform within their constraints
> and show very little creativity; they're not prepared to push the boat out.
> Then it needs a lot of diplomacy and tact to avoid head-to-head criticism
> and misunderstanding of intentions. But although there can be a lot of
> frustrations that come about because of your beliefs and what you feel to
> be important there is still room for a huge amount of personal growth in
> a non-authoritative leadership position.

This is not what is generally recognized as the language of 'male' leadership informed by hegemonic patriarchal discourses which operates in commerce, industry and public institutions (Connell 2009). Such models have long been recognized as inappropriate to the early years sector (Kagan and Bowman 1997; Rodd 2006; Aubrey 2011). The experiences of Tom and Daniel support our contention that gender differences are a misleading basis for examining early years leadership and that there is little empirical evidence of gendered leadership styles (Muijs *et al.* 2004). *Leadership within* offers an analysis of leadership which recognizes that gender is merely one among many individual identities of childcare professionals which offer diversity and multiple ways of knowing. While male workers are very much in the minority the same could also be said of practitioners with disabilities and, to a lesser extent, those from ethnically diverse backgrounds. There are no debates about the different approach or style of these practitioners but their alternative ways of knowing contribute in the same way to the politics of occupational identity (Moss 2006). The relevance of male leadership in early years therefore lies not in a supposed gendered style of leading but in their different ways of being professional. Alternative ways of being point to multiple knowledges by which practitioners can engage in a critical pedagogy (Freire 1999) and bring an ethical and democratic dimension to early years practice (Dahlberg and Moss 2005; Moss 2010). Leadership lies in the readiness to re-examine values, challenging self and others, and this potential is immanent within any practitioner, regardless of gender or other identity, whose sense of social purpose and mission is underpinned by reflective integrity.

Reflective prompts

1   What is the prime motivation for Tom and Daniel in the leadership they display? In what ways is their leadership affected by their gender?
2   Choose an aspect of your professional identity and examine how it can impact on the way you operate in practice.

6 Enthused and empowered: inner relational interdependence

Relationships are a central feature of much of the leadership literature (Sergiovanni 1998, 2001; Harris 2008). Traditionally leadership has been seen as something exercised over others and so the kind of interpersonal skills likely to encourage colleagues to follow have been considered essential for effective leadership. Within ECEC, relationships are usually viewed in a rather different light, with emphasis on developing respectful and constructive relationships with others considered a valuable goal in itself and not simply 'oiling the wheels' for practical, operational reasons. The importance attached to relationships with all individuals – children, parents and carers, and other professionals both within the setting and beyond – is asserted in policies and frameworks such as the *Early Years Foundation Stage* (DfES 2008), the *Children's Plan* (DCSF 2007) and the last two *Children Acts* (DoH1989; DfES 2004). Our paradigm takes this early years values-based ethos as the guide for interpersonal relationships which cultivate and enable *leadership within*.

Leadership and relationships

The fact that ECEC is founded on a culture of valuing reciprocal relationships does not mean that the traditional leader/follower divide does not exist in the sector. Avery (2004) has suggested that unless it is specifically contextualized, people have a tendency to hold command and control as their basic leadership model. The influence of unexamined concepts of leadership lurks in our subconscious and continues to affect our attitudes, beliefs and actions unless they are challenged. This can make it difficult for early years practitioners to think of themselves as leaders or recognize what they do on a daily basis as leadership. The hegemony of authority-based leadership models means taken-for-granted assumptions shape the organization and working relationships of most settings. As a result those who hold positions of authority such as manager, deputy or room leader are expected, by their colleagues and themselves, to direct the practice of others. Understandings of leadership are usually unrecognized and unquestioned, which may leave nominated leader(s) wholly responsible for direction and innovation within the setting while other practitioners can find themselves limited to more passive and subservient roles. The paradigm of *leadership within* challenges such delineated responsibilities so that leadership can be seen as a shared and collaborative process. This is reflected in the feature of *relational interdependence* that recognizes the connectivity of individuals so that an organization can be viewed as an entire system rather than a grouping of separate beings. Such connectivity and interdependence does not simply happen but needs proactive intention and effort; even when practitioners know each other well as part of a long-standing team they may still find themselves working in parallel rather than taking part in a collective undertaking.

The introduction of Early Years Professional Status (EYPS) in England formalized a role for graduate professionals first recommended more than two decades ago in the Rumbold Report (DES1990). The Children's Workforce Development Council (CWDC) designated the role of EYPs as leaders of practice and assessment for the award of the status is dependent on demonstrating leadership of others (CWDC 2010). Given the common assumptions already noted about leadership, it is understandable that this may sometimes cause a quandary for practitioners who, though confident in their own practice and the importance of their contribution within their settings, may be less sure about how this relates to leadership. It has been evident to us as EYP providers that default concepts of control and command leadership can often undermine candidates' self-perception so that we may need to support and empower them to examine preconceptions, challenge previously uncontested notions and thus re-envisage leadership (McDowall Clark in press). Exploring and debating concepts of leadership benefits those who are not in recognized positions of authority who can begin to appreciate for themselves the ways in which they lead practice; it also enables practitioners with formal responsibilities to review the generally unexamined ideas behind their own roles. The leadership profile discussed in this chapter is based on extracts from reflective accounts of practice written by one candidate, June, while she was undertaking EYPS and reflecting on the leadership in her role. June is the deputy manager of a private nursery situated in a large market town who embarked on her Foundation degree three years ago. She works mainly with the toddler age group and was in the process of completing a full honours degree when she began EYPS.

Developing a community

If it is to be successful then leadership must be concerned with creating an effective community (Rodd 2006); this points to the need for connectivity and relational interdependence. June's appreciation of this was evident in a group discussion when she remarked:

> It's not just about making relationships with parents myself; the staff all need to be involved – we're all making relationships all the time. So by working together on a bigger stage we can be so much more effective.

June appreciates the benefits of mutuality and the necessity of this if change is to be sustained and have a lasting impact – her comment demonstrates a focus on participation rather than her own personal agenda. Such participation may need to be nurtured so that all practitioners can feel confident to make an active, valued and relevant contribution. This is not always straightforward; it is more complicated and demanding to develop participatory ways of working than it is to take charge and instruct others (Lambert 2002) but June's commitment to the participation of the whole staff team is evident in her reflection on reviewing policy. Although as deputy manager she acknowledges that she has responsibility for writing up policy and keeping an overview of planning across the nursery, the practice outlined in the new policy emerges from a collaborative process.

> As well as reviewing and modifying our setting's existing policies and procedures I worked in collaboration with the manager and other colleagues to develop a new one. Our 'Growing Together through the Early Years Foundation Stage' policy discusses the new framework that we work with. It talks about our short, medium and long-term planning that I have implemented across our setting looking at the four themes and commitments of the EYFS and what we aim to achieve through them all. One of the themes I carefully considered and reflected on while developing the policy was 'Learning and Development'. I gave thought to the play experiences we provide in our nursery like messy play, sensory experiences, story, role play, ICT and music and came to the conclusion that although these experiences are good they could be better. After a meeting and discussion everyone agreed and showed great enthusiasm with an idea that arose. It was decided that to enhance the quality of what we provide, different staff members would be in charge of each of the play experiences, these staff members being called area development officers (ADOs).
>
> I have provided some training for development officers in their area to gain new ideas, thoughts and skills to make sure new and stimulating resources are provided. They also visit the rest of the departments to observe how much children and staff are getting out of the experience. These staff members then provide rooms with feedback from their

observations and suggest next steps to enhance play experiences further. Observations are carried out in each room every month and in between new resources and equipment are purchased if necessary. Each area development officer has produced a folder with observations, photos and a resource list that can be viewed by everyone to see how children are enjoying and achieving with the enhanced play opportunities. Staff members have been very happy to take charge of an area of play and it is clear that they have been very enthused and empowered by it. It is because of them and through the help of colleagues that they have made the play experiences more fun, exciting and beneficial for the children. Observing has also been a good way to allow staff members to move around a little to see what other rooms and age groups are doing as, being such a large and busy nursery, staff haven't always been able to do this.

The moral valuing of colleagues (Canning 2009) is an essential element of ethical leadership and June displays this in her concern to include all staff in developing a Foundation Stage policy. This is not simply a matter of delegation, which is a recognized aspect of traditional authoritarian leadership, but is integral to a facilitative and collaborative approach. In this way, all the practitioners are included in the co-construction of the environment and as a result are more likely to share June's commitment and motivation. Formulating policy could be considered a pragmatic area for co-construction to ensure consistency of approach and that all staff are fully conversant with the setting's policies and procedures. The co-construction of the environment in June's setting, however, goes beyond the immediately practical by facilitating mutual learning opportunities through which practitioners learn from each other and can all contribute to improving practice. June recognizes how staff have been 'enthused and empowered' by this and so demonstrates the importance of relational interdependence in improving practice. Her own enthusiasm drives her desire to extend this empowerment further:

I am the ADO for heuristic play which I am thoroughly enjoying. I have found out more about its history and am already seeing the benefits to the children in playing this way. I have found it really interesting buying and collecting appealing objects and seeing the enjoyment of the children through my observations.

As heuristic play is new to the setting I have shared what I've found and its benefits for the children with parents and carers. I've done this by showing the resources first hand at a parents' evening and displaying a poster and photos in the foyer. The benefits of involving parents and carers in helping us to collect equipment were great. It allowed them to understand heuristic play and also meant that families' cultures and backgrounds were respected as many different objects were shared, looked at and explored. It has also empowered parents to become involved in our curriculum and work with us and may have provided them with new ideas for play opportunities at home too.

A 'small step' approach

June's role with the toddlers prompted her to take on the development of heuristic play within the setting. Heuristic play exploring open-ended objects is particularly suited to this age group (Goldschmied and Jackson 2004) and a clear connection is evident between the development of such play opportunities and the review of play experiences to support learning and development which June has already mentioned. Beneficial as heuristic play is, however, it is not this outcome that shows her leadership as much as the process of relational interdependence of which it is a part. June appreciates that individual action is insufficient for sustained change and works to involve the active contribution of all stake holders. She recognizes that innovation can only be successful if everybody has ownership and her leadership exists not in telling others what to do but in engaging them in the process so that they can contribute their different strengths and expertise.

> Just from a small change that was made while reviewing our policies and procedures a huge difference was created throughout the whole setting. Through being proactive I have managed to empower parents and carers to contribute to our curriculum and work in partnership with us; staff members have joined in with my enthusiasm to take charge of their own area of play and enhance it and this has resulted in higher quality experiences being provided. Children have also been encouraged to gain new skills which in turn have encouraged their self-esteem and confidence.
>
> As Deputy Manager I have carried through the ADO idea and been part of it myself to model my enthusiasm and motivation to make new experiences for children as exciting as possible. I've been able to share with my colleagues the positive results of working with parents and shared my observations and new objects (resources) with them. I've also visited different rooms to share heuristic play with everybody and this has brought colleagues closer together as a working team.

Here June demonstrates what Canning refers to as 'a "practitioner-centred" approach which echoes the ethos and values of relationships with children' (2009: 34). She recognizes that much has come about 'just from a small change' and indeed this small steps approach is more likely to bring about sustainable improvement (McDowall Clark and Baylis 2011). Although June identifies the source of this change in the creation of ADOs, it could equally be put down to the impetus created by reviewing policies and procedures as a staff team or some quite different root such as her own and others' reflections about practice. Ultimately it does not really matter where change initiates from because it is the *process* of leadership rather than individual activities which are important. This is apparent in the comments of an early years mentor for the Foundation degree students discussing the impact of reflection on practice and the consequent leadership which emerges as a result:

> I see lots of change from when I started visiting settings and it's often difficult to put your finger on just why. Often it's starting from very basic things like reorganizing a room so as to get the best from it – and then from that [the students I mentor] will go on to develop different areas within the room. It can seem very simple but it still has an effect on the whole and things change as a result. For instance, in one of my settings there was a monumental change and I said to them 'This is completely different – why is that? What has happened?' There hadn't been any change in the staff but there had been a change in people's responsibility – and as result everything changed. [Foundation degree practitioner students] have enabled it to happen but not necessarily acknowledged why – they don't give themselves the credit which is due to them when change occurs.

This echoes June's comment about how 'just a small change' can have a very large impact. The mentor suggests that practitioners may be slow to give themselves credit for the changes which they bring about – a consequence of default models of leadership whereby practitioners may not recognize what they do as leadership because it does not match their concept of what a leader does. On the other hand, taking individual credit is perhaps not a helpful way of looking at change and points to the value of a new paradigm of leadership which can inform different ways of working and the value of relational interdependence.

Leadership within does not rely on invested power, so although June occupies the role of deputy manager she is less concerned with pushing her own perspective than with encouraging the involvement of others. In this way, she is able to support the potential contribution of her colleagues by fostering relational interdependence which then becomes a strength of the entire group. As we saw with the example of heuristic play, it is not the outcome but the process which matters, demonstrating the importance of professional dialogue in enabling and sustaining relational interdependence. As June is currently doing her degree she is keen to disseminate among her colleagues the new ideas she is coming across. The synthesis between different factors of *leadership within* is evident in the way in which June's recognition of the importance of relational interdependence is prompted by reflective integrity:

Session lectures at university allowed me to explore creativity, creative dispositions and ways of being creative in action and this has broadened my views of what being creative entails. I have always thought of creativity as being all about the imagination as children work with media, also how they can use and develop their senses, but through discussions and reflection I now realize how much else is entailed. Creativity is the expression of ideas in a personal and unique way. . .Creativity for both myself and the children allows expression and effective communication; we are allowed to think outside the box and take risks in order to develop learning without feeling a failure. Creativity also promotes happiness as while we are allowed to be flexible and experiment we are being enthusiastic, motivated and able to show our unique flairs. I reflected on whether or not I am a creative individual and whether I can offer more creative values to the children within my setting.

As deputy manager I have to problem solve frequently and experiment with new ideas; I have to listen and respond to all staff and use their feedback as well as that of parents and carers to reflect upon our practice continually, and think about changes that could be made to ensure our provision is one of quality. I have to play with ideas, to imagine possibilities and to analyse problems. As deputy manager I have to be able to think outside the box 'divergently' as well as narrowly in a 'convergent' way.

Although I used to think that being reflective and creative are very different I am now starting to see how they are interlinked. Qualities for both are very similar and I think I display a lot of these. I think everybody could be creative and many people are without realizing. It is perhaps down to personality, beliefs and values that decide how creative we are and our path of learning, people we have learnt from and training we have received. In reflecting on this I wondered whether it is these values and beliefs that can sometimes restrain some children from being creative, for instance telling them that something has to be used for a particular purpose!

I had a long hard think about my setting and how we nurture creativity in children. We already provide open-ended resources for exploratory play and investigation and a rich range of materials and resources. On the other hand I do think staff would benefit from me cascading my new learning about creativity to see the importance of allowing more time and freedom and also to let children take risks and develop their own learning styles.

Staff members in our setting also display different levels of creativity, all of which are beneficial in different situations, some with great imagination skills and others who are good with problem solving. We have logical thinkers and some who are more willing to take risks and others who have artistic flair. We discussed this in a staff meeting to give examples of how we are all different and it was a great way to recognize and praise the different qualities of the staff members.

I have understood from this experience the importance of cascading my new knowledge and ideas with others and feel more confident doing so. Our setting cannot be effectively run with one person; we are a team and communication is imperative. I am lucky enough to be at university gaining new knowledge that can benefit all staff members and not just myself.

June shows recognition that change and improvement cannot come from an individual working alone. She appreciates the different attributes of others and how these can all contribute to the setting. She also demonstrates catalytic agency in her willingness to bring this about – not in the sense of persuading or going ahead to show the way but rather through respecting individuals and their own strengths and perspectives. June is keen to empower others, seeking commonalities and recognizing the complementarity of other practitioners rather than pushing her own views. Her enthusiasm comes from the excitement she clearly derives from her own learning and professional development, a motive which draws on professional passion, as she explains:

> It's definitely passion, the reason why you do it in the first place and why you want to empower others. Everyone needs empowering and by doing that you're giving them the passion.
>
> (Group discussion among EYP candidates)

This professional passion (Taggart 2011; Murray in press) and the enthusiasm it engenders prompts leadership independently of positional power as practitioners take responsibility for improving practice themselves and nurture the ability of others to do so too. June recognizes the potential of her colleagues to show leadership also and thereby change the role of practitioner beyond 'a series of task-based occupations and towards the idea of a critical thinking, creative, team working professional' (Cameron 2004: 19). By undertaking degree-level study June has come to the realization that her leadership does not derive from her position as deputy manager but is manifest in her critical thinking and her passion to make a difference. This indicates the strong connection between leadership and learning which our paradigm of *leadership within* emphasizes. Lave and Wenger (1991) differentiate between conventional notions of 'learning by doing' and communities of practice (echoed in Cameron's distinction between 'task-based occupations' and critical thinking professionals above); it is the latter sense of constructive, shared learning that underpins relational interdependence.

Leading partnerships

If learning is conceptualized as a socio-cultural practice (Lave and Wenger 1991) it is evident that this forms the common purpose at the core of ECEC; work with children, staff, parents and carers is all focused on the same goals to the extent that it is founded on the fundamental purpose of learning. This makes partnership extremely important and it is clearly integral to relational interdependence. June demonstrates a strong sense of partnership, not only with her colleagues and other practitioners but in her genuine respect and desire to work with parents and families, as was evident in the way she shared practice regarding heuristic play. Another example of wider partnership demonstrates the relational interdependence at the heart of June's leadership within her setting:

> Parents coming to look around the nursery asked June about her ability to care appropriately for their 2-year-old son, Ben, who has phenyl-ketonuria (PKU). June had only ever come across one other child with this condition but shared what she knew – that it is an enzyme deficiency that prevents the breakdown of protein in the body. His parents were reassured that June was prepared to ensure Ben's well-being and booked him in for a number of settling-in visits. Meanwhile June researched PKU thoroughly and prepared background information sheets for the rest of the team because she knew that if the condition is not handled very carefully it can lead to mental illness. She was concerned to ensure everything was done to safeguard Ben while also ensuring his full inclusion in the activities of the nursery. During the settling-in period June had regular discussions with Ben's mother to clarify which foods he could eat, which he could have in moderation and what must be avoided – as she said, 'It was important to look at the individual healthy diet I could offer this child and not only focus on what I couldn't!' June introduced the mother to the nursery cook so they could collaborate on menus and planning and asked if she might invite Ben's dietician along to deliver some training. Mum also attended that training so she could fill in gaps about her child's routines and habits. On the basis of all this preparatory work Ben settled easily into nursery and was able to sit alongside the other children for snacks and mealtimes. Collaboration with the mother meant he could regularly take part in cooking sessions – for instance, Ben was excited to be able to bring in some of his 'special' milk to share with the other children so they could all make porridge together.

As we have argued, *leadership within* is concerned with the process of leadership rather than specific tasks and activities. The particular details of this situation in terms of meeting a child's individual needs and his or her transition to nursery are thus simply the outward symptom of June's awareness of the relational interdependence of all who are involved in the work of the setting. So leadership potential can be present within any situation because it is not part of the specific behaviour but of the meaning behind it (Rosemary and Puroila 2002). June recognized that in order to ensure good practice in line with her own values and those of the nursery it would be necessary for everybody to work together and that this partnership must include not only other early childhood practitioners but also Ben's mum, the hospital dietician and the cook so that everyone could contribute and learn from each other. This recognition prompted June to rethink her ideas about staff training and the purpose behind this in a constructive and mutually dependent way for the benefit of the child.

> [T]he need for staff training is not just to get a certificate or have a bit more knowledge but for them to feel more confident and assertive in different areas. Training is essential to encourage new and fresh thinking and it also helps other practitioners to gain the experience and confidence to work with outside professionals.

This reinforces June's drive to establish an active learning community so that learning extends far beyond basic 'training' opportunities and becomes genuine professional development.

Making it happen

Relational interdependence requires work and proactive engagement. In this way, it is very dependent on the other features of *leadership within*, namely catalytic agency and reflective integrity. June's own reflection on her learning prompts a desire to make a difference and bring about improvements and in this she demonstrates her agency as a catalyst within her setting. Leadership is situational in nature (Hujala 2002) and so *leadership within* may be demonstrated by any practitioner who is self-aware and committed to making a difference. Commitment and self-awareness provides the motivation to reflect on experiences as they arise and to consider the impact of actions and events on others. For instance, talking to her manager about the introduction of EYFS into the setting led June to become more aware of her own thoughts about leadership and the importance of involving other people.

> I thought about such a confident professional being nervous about changes and it made me realize how much less confident nursery assistants must feel when change is initiated all the time and put to them from leaders and managers! I can see how important it is to empower these

people, especially to get involved in meetings and feedback to put across their views and feelings and to help lead change also.

This [discussion] made me reflect a great deal on myself as an agent of change, on who I involve as a leader and how I can empower my own team to be involved in leading change so that they can feel a sense of achievement, enthused and motivated. It also helped me realize the benefit of listening to others and how it is up to me to listen, help and guide others, taking them on journeys of their own in order to empower them. It became apparent to me that my dispositions and attitude have a lot to do with early years professionalism. I have learned how the perceptions I form of others are very important and I recognize how it is imperative that I act as an agent of change myself and that I work with others and continue to reflect on practice, training and new learning. If I don't do this and never want to change myself then I will never be able to change what goes on around me. And if I don't change what goes on around me then I am not helping anybody as I will not be looking to enhance daily practice and enjoying working with others to reap the satisfaction of what we do.

Relational interdependence is a strength of effective early years settings and June is working hard to develop this. Whereas in traditional authoritarian leadership situations the role of the individual leader in charge is crucial, so much so that if that person leaves his or her post then the organization may struggle to continue until a replacement is found, relational interdependence creates a network that maintains its own momentum. While it may initially be more complicated to work in a participative manner and to create a sense of relational interdependence than it would be to simply take charge and instruct others, ultimately the most effective leadership is that which empowers others in an environment in which everyone takes responsibility for mutual learning. Such leadership enables the development of a genuine community of learners committed not only to personal development but, through this, to the development of their setting and of the wider community. June's own sense of inner leadership supports her as an active agent of change so that she is confident in her own position and does not feel threatened or challenged in any way by the competence and ability of others. Her recognition of the complementary abilities and potential of other practitioners means that she uses her position to empower others rather than to direct them, welcoming and encouraging their strengths and diversity. In this way, her leadership is true *leadership within*, not dependent on invested power as the deputy manager but demonstrated through her inner commitment to developing and sustaining a nurturing and productive work context, one in which every individual is able to make an active contribution and to share in the process of leadership.

Reflective prompts

1 June's leadership does not lie in the exertion of authority but in the way in which she uses her position to engage in leadership processes. What is it about her approach that enables this to happen?

2 How does June demonstrate her belief in the potential of others to engage in shared pedagogical practice so as to develop relational interdependence and a learning community?

3 Consider your own strengths and aptitudes within your role. How can you foster conditions for relational interdependence in the way in which you work?

7 Letting go of ownership: the diffusion of catalytic agency

Group culture and identity develop over time so that it might be claimed that organizations are created by the people within them (Bush 2003). Their culture is the product of interaction between individuals who share a common purpose or interests and over time this becomes embedded in practices and procedures. To that extent an organizational culture can be 'mindless', that is, habitual and unquestioned, unless its members are prepared to cast off institutionalized thought and allow principle rather than precedent to guide their thinking. The context in which leadership develops is therefore significant if an organization is to become dynamic rather than static. Dynamic leadership is most often conceptualized as positional, residing in a strong head with the power to take an organization forward. The power involved need not be the traditional power of command, it may be inspirational and act through persuasion; nonetheless, although a clear distinction exists between positional power and personal power, both reside in *personhood*. The dynamic leadership which emerges within a community of practitioners, however, operates beyond the individual to create a mindful organization that takes mutual responsibility for the co-construction of meaning and direction (Sergiovanni 2001). Such an organization can be said to be displaying catalytic agency.

Catalytic agency does not simply spring into existence out of nowhere; its source is in the strong professional values which underpin a common purpose. In the case of early years professionals, this lies in a commitment to the welfare of young children and their families (Moyles 2001; Taggart 2011). Such an ethic of care creates the necessary emotional climate for leadership to flourish. Goleman *et al.* (2002) term this emotional quality 'resonance', which acknowledges the significance of the affective domain in securing people's desire for and commitment to collective action. Within ECEC the emotional resonance of the work is usually the motivation and incentive behind practitioners' choice of career (Murray in press).

The growth of leadership from emotional connection rather than to serve an instrumental purpose is particularly applicable to *leadership within* and functioning at a collective level can demonstrate how leadership is more usefully conceptualized as a process, as something which evolves and is created, rather than as a personal attribute attached to specific people and roles. Organizations which exhibit catalytic agency are dynamic in nature and always on the brink of change and improvement. Such change, however, is experienced as motivating and exciting rather than frightening or inhibiting – as one practitioner put it, 'We're not there yet – but it's *nice* to not be there yet!'

Reggio Emilia as a starting point for catalytic agency

Diffused catalytic agency can be a very powerful force when organizations assume shared and collective responsibility and work in a pro-active, self-managing manner to bring about change. This is exemplified in the way that a loose network of settings has taken inspiration from the Reggio Emilia approach to develop practice among their community in an area of south-west England. A number of practitioners initially visited Reggio on a study visit but the influence of this experience has since spread considerably further than their own individual practice because of the resonance of the approach with both personal and collective values. As Nina recalls:

> I first got interested in Reggio when I saw the travelling exhibition 'The Hundred Languages of Children' some years ago now. It really caught me because it was what I'd always believed in so it gave me permission to work in a certain kind of way. Since then others have come along who believe in the same things and so that is very much how we work with the children, researching with them. Children are always asking questions; they want to know about something so we go and find out together.

Although it was the way in which Reggio values resonated with her own which first attracted Nina to find out more, the practice in the children's centre where she works has now moved beyond that initial influence to develop a collective approach. A mutual value base gives confidence to all of the practitioners, enabling them to develop a shared purpose which is particular to that setting rather than an adaptation of something else. The way in which values, mission and purpose synthesize to create something new in response to local circumstances is also evident in another centre in the same area where Marie says:

> Although the rest of the staff here haven't been to Reggio they are all very interested in the approach and the underlying principles – they all do lots of research and reading – and I suppose in a way they really

bought into my 'vision'. So of course now it's no longer *my* vision – it's been completely overtaken by them all, which is right.

The way in which this setting is a dynamic organization is evident in how the direction develops among practitioners as a whole rather than being imposed by an individual. This diffused catalytic agency engenders new ideas and new directions and becomes self-generating so that individual practitioners derive their satisfaction from a shared undertaking rather than through personal control. The examples shown here illustrate how the diffused element of *leadership within* differs noticeably from the distributed leadership model previously recommended for ECEC (Ebbeck and Waniganayake 2003; Siraj-Blatchford and Manni 2007). Diffused leadership is not distributed or handed out to individuals who then commit to certain tasks or roles; rather it is a shared dynamic which builds impetus and momentum from and in itself. It is notable that Marie states that the rest of the staff team are involved in 'lots of research and lots of reading'; diffused leadership develops in an environment in which individuals are keen to learn and extend their knowledge. The professional fervour prompted by joint learning and exploration of ideas is evident when Marie talks about her initial visit to Reggio Emilia:

> I went to visit Reggio with work colleagues and other nursery staff – at the time I worked in a different setting – so it was fantastic to go as a team to experience it all. Not that there was anything new in the fact that children benefit from the outdoors and like to play with open-ended objects, but it was lovely to experience the differences and share our thoughts – What are we going to do back home with these ideas? I loved the thinking, why they encouraged children to explore at their own pace, especially with my particular interest in special needs. They had a really interesting approach – they did the same sort of things but in a different way.

It is this interest in different ways of doing the same sort of things that generates catalytic agency at a diffused level. Although diffused leadership calls for a common purpose and shared values, this does not mean a rejection of challenge and multiple perspectives; indeed, reflection on diversity feeds the co-construction of knowledge. In this way we can see the interplay of the three features of leadership within – catalytic agency, reflective integrity and relational interdependence – which work together so that differing perspectives can be recognized and ambiguity or conflict become accepted as a part of learning. Reflective integrity operating at both an individual and an organizational level prompts agency among the different practitioners so that everyone has 'potential and capacity to influence and lead another' (Rosemary and

Puroila 2002: 15). Although Marie uses the term 'vision' to describe her philosophy, this is used in the sense of an 'ideal' of how things might be done differently. It is not at all the same thing as traditional 'visionary leadership' (Avery 2004), by which an individual leader inspires others by the force of their personality or charisma to buy into their ideas and carry out a predefined purpose. Marie is happy that it is no longer 'her' vision which provides direction but a collective and shared vision of practice:

> It was a fantastic opportunity with the total refurbishment of this building. We could put in curves instead of sharp corners and really think about the lay out. We've tried to keep it all very airy, for instance with the long corridor which had been very narrow, we were able to widen it considerably. The children love to run up and down it! And we've made sure there are lots of mirrors, lots of plants, and above all, space. The garden was a real bonus. And it's interesting how it's developed because I think we're all equal here in how we work and the contribution that everyone makes. So Jay, who's doing her Foundation degree at the moment, took the lead on the garden because of her skills and abilities. I think you need to be confident. . .but it's so important. . .letting go of ownership and enabling everyone to play their part. The whole education system seems to be about putting your name to things – that piece of work is yours, this one's mine. The whole of society too seems to be similar. So it's great to be able to. . .support something very creative and then other people realize all that they have the ability to do. It can seem alien at first because we always want to be accountable and have our name above the door but I think that. . .as a team you all grow hugely.

Shared values and shared ownership

The lack of 'ownership' which Marie identifies is crucial to catalytic agency operating at any level. On an individual basis a practitioner who consistently draws attention to his or her role not only runs the risk of irritating and antagonizing colleagues but also undermines the latent capacity of others; this offsets any potential to act as a catalyst in the setting. In terms of diffused leadership ownership becomes irrelevant; new thoughts are sparked through engagement with ideas and grow through discussion so it is likely that any eventual outcome will have no identifiable source, rather as a piece of knitting holds together through many individual stitches to create a whole garment out of a single thread.

Catalytic agency working at a diffused level therefore embodies leadership as a process and, rather than having one leader who controls and instructs, the organization itself can be seen as 'leaderful' (Raelin 2003), generating its own leadership and direction. For an organization to be leaderful all of its members need to be committed to a common purpose, not necessarily to be in complete accord about details but to share an overall ethic and purpose. Nina emphasizes the importance of this in connection with other practitioners sharing a similar attitude to working with the children:

> Some staff just can't do it. We always talk about [the Reggio approach] at interview but they just can't seem to do it – they have to tell the children what to do! But then we have to say to them – we're working here for the children, it's not for us and we're not going to change our way of working for you!

While ongoing debates about practice maintain a healthy level of challenge and critical analysis, if there is no underlying sharing of values then the potential for diffused catalytic agency will be impeded. Individuals hold their own personal philosophy, developed as a result of their education or training and their professional experience; this gives meaning to their decisions and is what governs their practice. A dynamic organization supports discussion with others through which a shared pedagogical view emerges which has meaning for all. Nivala (2002: 19) suggests that action must first be meaningful to individuals and then their commitment to mutual undertaking 'is thus clearly a more profound experience than an external promise given to the working community or a social sanction imposed by the organization'. In this way, the participative and shared process of leadership is embedded within the organizational culture. Marie recognizes this when she considers the impact of group dynamics on the learning process both within the organization and beyond:

> We've been very fortunate – throughout three years developing the team, and then 18 months ago we opened this centre, we've only lost one person, so the turnover is very low. . .but in the end one just hopes to choose wisely – they have to have a sense of humour! If staff come to work somewhere like this, there is a certain ethos. They are very motivated; we are always thinking about things and discussing them, we bounce ideas off each other all the time. For instance, just now there is someone delivering training, something they've just been to and so they're sharing it with the others. If they buy into the ethos then it is easier, a bit like families perhaps. We're fortunate to have universal services here and we find that families seem to learn from each other and pick things up – and the same applies to the staff too. . .And it certainly seems to be working from the reports we get back from other professionals. They recognize what it is we are trying to achieve. So we do share everything – it's not about any one person at all, so if someone has an idea they share it with all of us and we'll

say, 'OK, who wants to take this on?' It means there are always lots of opportunities so it's very exciting!

The shared responsibility for both formal and informal learning which is evident here demonstrates how closely aligned are learning and leadership within a diffused model of catalytic agency. This notion refutes the traditional image of ECEC as a low-level occupation for young girls with limited education (Colley 2006) and reinforces the role of early years practitioners as autonomous and accountable professionals seeking deeper understanding and new knowledge (Moss 2006; McDowall Clark and Baylis 2011).

Leadership diffused among the community

As in Reggio Emilia itself, the mutual meaning-making and reciprocal learning extends beyond the setting itself into the wider community. Marie recognizes that families also 'buy into the ethos' in the same way as practitioners, so that it becomes a joint endeavour illustrating the way that catalytic agency works in conjunction with relational interdependence. At her setting there is a growing number of people from the community, volunteers, families and grandparents, who are involved in working with the centre. She says, 'They're really enthusiastic. . .so I'm excited about the possibilities. We can offer so much more with a bigger work base.' An organization displaying catalytic agency can therefore spread beyond its own boundaries to become diffused within the mesosystem (Bronfenbrenner 1979). Nivala (2002: 19) proposes that early years leadership must have a strong presence within the mesosystem and suggests the fact that 'educational co-operation is part of the organizational culture' is essential to the character of leadership in the sector. That this leadership is both diffused and catalytic is evident when Marie explains how they work with a range of other settings such as private nurseries and primary schools:

> We have six early years settings that come to access our facilities which is really good because we can encourage our beliefs and vision more widely. And we do outreach with five different 'Stay and Play' sessions in community village halls. We're also setting up a parenting programme in one of the outlying villages. We go into nursery settings too and primary schools, to provide activities if they're feeling a little less confident, to show the way and support others. I think it's really important (certainly with the Stay and Play) because for some families it can be hugely difficult to walk through the door – there can still be a certain stigma attached. Accessing their local church hall is not so daunting, so it's a high priority for us to take opportunities out there.

Like Marie, Nina is also concerned that the catalytic agency latent in the organization becomes diffused among a wider community:

> We have a values day every month. The children choose the value and we make sure we do it first thing in the morning so there's always a lot of parents hanging around still. All the children are in the piazza and we get out the step ladder and choose the value for the month. We discuss how we can use this value through the month – for instance, this month it's friendship, making relationships, being kind to each other, making friends with children who are on their own, that sort of thing. We say to the parents if there's anything you can do at home to support this then we'd be really grateful. We don't want to patronize parents although we do want them involved – so this helps them to focus on what we're doing and then hopefully they'll carry on at home. This is a Children's Centre so some of the parents need extra support and this is a way that we can support them without them feeling preached at. . .The values are spread through the whole provision.

'Doing Reggio': a stimulus for reflection

A view of the setting as the centre of a community involving children, parents and carers alongside practitioners is evident in both Nina's and Marie's accounts and stems from the Reggio philosophy which underpins their thinking about curriculum and practice. This functions in both settings as well as the wider local network of practitioners engaging with catalytic agency on a diffused level. The Reggio Emilia approach has grown out of very particular cultural values, socio-economic conditions and political influences (Edwards *et al.* 1993) and therefore it would not be appropriate to try to import its philosophy and practice wholesale and impose it on provision in the UK – indeed, Moss (2001: 125) insists that it is not a 'generalizable experience'. Nonetheless, a visit to Reggio provided an opportunity to see through a new lens and the impact of reflecting on 'the same sort of things but in a different way' worked as a stimulus to prompt thinking about the rationale behind their own practice. Marie is unequivocal that her setting does not attempt to replicate Reggio:

> We don't 'do' Reggio here – what we do is give children the space and lots of opportunities to take risks, to challenge themselves, to be enquiring, to be inquisitive with a multitude of materials – and that includes people as well as objects! And we do try to pass on our values to parents too. That's how our work is inspired by the principles of Reggio, but it's important to remember that it's not a package; one can't write a manual as if there is something to simply follow. Ultimately it's about

what do we want? What we want is children who are confident, who are articulate and are competent learners throughout their lives. And we believe this is a really good way to encourage all that in children – to give them the best possible opportunities to become competent learners to be able to succeed in life.

There is an important point to be drawn from this; whether or not provision in any of these settings resembles that of Reggio does not ultimately matter. The relevance of the initial visit to Reggio Emilia lies in the fact that it acted as a prompt for re-envisioning practice. Such a prompt, which may come from anywhere at any time, feeds the ongoing critical evaluation of practice which can be discerned in a team displaying catalytic agency. As part of this process, the original spark is likely to change many times so that the outcome has little resemblance to the starting point; hence the irrelevance of 'ownership'. What is crucial, though, is proactive practitioners with self-belief, confidence and a deep commitment to their moral and ethical purpose. To that extent finding out more about the Reggio approach stimulated leadership activity on a collective basis.

As ECEC becomes increasingly regulated and 'demands for performativity and technicist practice' (Osgood 2006a) act to constrain practitioners, then it is more important than ever that organizations can deploy leadership in the form of catalytic agency to engage in constructive critique.

Nina too said that Reggio 'gave her permission' to work in a certain way and how this has developed is evident when she describes how practice is organized in her setting:

> We do [everything] in our own particular way! For instance, we set up for every age group and it depends how they want to use it – babies or 4-year-olds use things in a different context. The children use [space and resources] as they need to, depending on their stage of development. The curriculum talks about specific age groups but it's quite hard to focus on how to do that because lots of younger children do the same things too. It does come with problems of course – health and safety issues if toddlers are with the babies or pre-school for instance. They learn to negotiate and they may get knocked over! We share the garden (we do have a baby garden but we don't just use it for them, we use it a lot for craftwork and things like that) so the garden is a chance for brothers and sisters to be together. It's brilliant for transitions and moving from one room to another is never a problem because they're used to it. It's all free flow and if a baby crawls into the nursery it's no problem – and there's lots of stuff for them to watch! So when they come to 'move on' they've explored already. It's still the same ratios and everybody is everybody's! We do have key workers and they are responsible for Learning Journeys

and they liaise with parents but if they are outside, say, then they are responsible for those children. If more children go outside then someone else goes out and staff deploy themselves appropriately. So the children know all the staff well.

The underlying principles of the Reggio approach are evident here; the child is viewed as 'rich in potential, strong, competent and powerful' (Malaguzzi 1996: 117) and there is recognition that children are active in their own learning and learn through interacting with the environment and people around them. The concern though is not to take on the most easily replicated surface aspects of Reggio whereby they become simply 'reproducers of someone else's knowledge' (Moss 2001: 132) but to use these principles to develop practice appropriate to the setting and the children within it. As Nina continues:

At circle time we have three groups which are more or less of an age or ability – for instance, we have a boy who's nearly 4 and he goes with the 2-year-olds because its more developmentally appropriate for him. He has a possible language disorder and needs lots of support. He's happy and confident in there but would lose confidence with the older group where the children are telling stories and so on. He may be able to go into mainstream with support – we don't know yet – so we work with him and try to give him what he needs. Life isn't rigid – it changes all the time, so flexibility is necessary. We all of us, children and adults, go in different directions.

The confidence in their own values which has emerged through diffused catalytic agency enables practitioners in Nina's setting to challenge the traditional organization of age groups and abilities which inform the official curriculum. Too often normative developmental stages and milestones assume quasi-scientific status (Burman 2001) which then shapes practice and provision to the detriment of children who struggle to fit such mythic norms. To challenge such expectations and work differently requires questioning and self-managing practitioners and, while it is clearly not the only route to diffused catalytic agency, 'Reggio Emilia is. . .one of many examples of local islands of dissension, whose very existence proves the possibility to think and act differently' (Moss 2006: 39).

Agency and process

Thinking and acting differently is a dynamic process which must be constantly negotiated by a 'mindful' organization, but this is not always straightforward, as Marie points out:

Of course, all the time we're governed by frameworks and these demand particular end products so in a way we have to play games in order to achieve the necessary outcomes – for instance, to satisfy Ofsted. So in fact, these things can get in the way of the process, or rather, of being able to focus on the process – they do get in the way if you're not careful.

Focusing on the process is a crucial element of *leadership within* and a central function of organizations displaying catalytic agency. This enables pedagogical leadership to come to the fore, as is evident when Nina explains the basis of their planning:

How we observe is really important – we look at what the children have done, what they've learned and link it to the EYFS – never the other way round. So we observe children and then plan from that for the opportunities that they're interested in. A common interest may go on for months or just a week – until it comes to its natural end. There are usually lots of mini projects going on at the same time – for instance at the moment they're really into wood work and attaching things. We're asking parents to bring in anything the children find interesting that they can attach. The staff record when a child says something – 'Oh, that looks like a rocket because. . .!' We don't have any final idea of where we will end up or how the children will interpret things but it all links in the end in the evaluations. The children plan for themselves – our role is to facilitate it all.

In contemporary society the growing influence of neo-liberal policies means child-centredness too easily becomes simply a rhetorical mantra which is easily overcome by the need to fulfil government targets and outcomes. Increased regulation to ensure 'quality provision' leading to 'successful outcomes' thus militates against pedagogical values and the ethics of care (McDowall Clark 2011). In such a climate there is a pressing need for questioning professionals to develop and maintain communities of practice (Wenger 1998) which can challenge 'outcome pedagogy' (Solway 2000, cited in Moss 2006). This requires clear-sighted and value-based leadership which is enacted collectively (Murray 2009). Diffused catalytic agency is the process whereby values, relational interdependence and democratic practice are acted out within a moral and ethical dimension. In this way individual settings and loose networks of early childhood organizations create sites of learning and democratic practice (Dahlberg and Moss 2005) which can encompass not only practitioners but also children, families and the wider community. New opportunities and possibilities open up when the process of leadership is diffused across a wider dimension so that joint agency can become the catalyst for innovation and development.

Reflective prompts

1   What values resonate for you in your practice? To what extent are these values shared and articulated among practitioners?
2   In what ways could you develop a sharing of values and purpose across the wider community?
3   For Marie and Nina a visit to Reggio Emilia provided a stimulus to look at things 'in a different way'. What could be a stimulus for your own use? How might you use such a stimulus?

8 Reflective integrity: a diffused social competence

In this chapter, a voluntary-based Children's Centre provides the material to illustrate reflective integrity operating across the whole organization, as a diffused dimension of leadership. Two scenarios are taken from participant observational data in real-life situations and have been amended to ensure anonymity and protect vulnerable persons, heeding ethical guidance on educational research (BERA 2004). These scenarios demonstrate how reflective integrity can become a way of working and learning collectively in a leadership process, regardless of roles or position. To understand the term reflective integrity and its place in the paradigm of *leadership within*, we will first explore the concepts of reflection and integrity more deeply to consider their interrelationship and meaning for leadership.

Reflection: cognition and emotion

Reflection is generally understood in the context of learning as a means to explore experience in order to gain new or greater understanding. It has a reputation 'for distilling rational knowledge from the mess of human experience' (Jordi 2011: 182). This view of reflection emerged historically from Dewey (1933), positing the need for critical inquiry of first-hand experience to test assumptions and create meaning for ourselves, showing reflection as intentional capacity to change.

Schön (1991) enhanced the place of reflection in professional practice by linking reflection with action. 'Through Schön's work, action became an integral part of reflection resulting in reflective practice' (Clarke *et al.* 2007: 18), and a number of models have been devised since to support the process of reflection and learning from experience. The purpose of reflective practice is often seen as gaining new knowledge which can be used to improve practice and justify or inform decisions and actions and, as such, it can be given a rationalist connotation (Jordi 2011). Kinsella (2010), however, called for more recognition of the intuitive and creative processes in knowledge creation. He draws attention to the way practitioners use tacit knowledge and reflection implicit in their actions as artistry in dealing with uncertainty, unique situations and value conflicts (Schön 1991). Part of Schön's legacy is that reflection in and on practice places the practitioner as an active agent, becoming part of the situation and helping to shape it, thus 'generating knowledge in the midst of practice' (Kinsella 2010: 568). This has particular significance for *catalytic agency* in leadership, as described in Chapters 4 and 7.

Subsequent development of more philosophical and psychological perspectives of reflection have viewed it as part of being human, having a cognitive existence and part of the natural process of trying to make sense of the world around us and understand ourselves (Clarke *et al.* 2007). Jordi (2011) argues that the historical development of ideas about reflection has placed too much emphasis on the cognitive domain, creating a mind–body duality which underplays the way in which thought and feeling integrate through experience. Calling on neuroscience, he argues that, just as the brain is part of the central nervous system, integration of thought and emotion is intrinsic to our thought processes, therefore we should allow feelings and emotions to be part of the reflective process. This allows 'dissonances' to come through which enable contradictions and tensions to be held or unresolved, more truly reflecting the rich and complex nature of human experience. Working with dissonance is a common leadership challenge and Scenario 1 provides an example of unresolved tensions in practice which were ameliorated through a collective process of reflection.

Leadership scenario 1: Internal review of a child protection case

The details of this case concerning child protection are not provided for ethical reasons but also because the significance for our study lies in the leadership process of self-review which the Children's Centre team initiated following the case. The team adopted reflective integrity as a way of working collectively through the 'messiness' of practice.

The Children's Centre was involved in a difficult child protection case, which concluded with a child being taken into care. The experience of the case left a general feeling of discomfiture among staff, a feeling of matters unresolved. The frontline practitioners expressed a need to release the emotional tensions built up through the case and a strong ethical sense of wanting to examine the integrity of their actions against their values and beliefs. The staff wanted to explore the case to express their feelings and concerns and reconcile actions with decisions taken, in order to check whether they had done all they could to protect the child. A key challenge emerged from a frontline practitioner, which was whether they had individually and collectively acted in tune with core values, keeping child welfare paramount.

The nominated safeguarding officer (NSO) welcomed the challenge, respecting the right of team members to do so and seeing the potential for learning from reflection. Whilst the NSO was experienced in safeguarding and had acted on that basis during the case, she recognized that tacit knowledge borne from experience needs checking for continuing validity and legitimacy. Consequently, they decided to conduct an internal review. This was not primarily a procedural review but a reflective review to enable all perspectives to be heard and to identify potential learning for the future.

There was common purpose in the review to identify what learning could be gained from the experience and discover ways in which practice could be further developed. A need for professional self-validation was at the heart of this, to reconcile thoughts and feelings with the events and actions that took place. The team asked themselves, could they individually or collectively have done anything differently or better? Was the child's welfare paramount at all times? Did they communicate effectively with each other, parents and external agencies?

Each staff member, involved in the case or affected by it, was invited to write privately their own reflective account as a chronology and distil from this what went well, not so well and what ideas they had for the future. The distilled perspectives were shared with each other and then a trusted mentor for the Centre, who had not been involved in the case, was asked to conduct the review. Each staff member talked through his or her account with the mentor and was encouraged to voice personal feelings, reasoning and concerns after which all staff affected by the case met to listen to the feedback and discuss the issues which emerged.

The practitioners directly involved in the daily interaction with the child and parents felt that tension had arisen within the team regarding the locus of problem, the severity, and what was in their power to resolve. The dilemma facing them was 'holding the situation', keeping sufficient trust with the family to ensure they kept attending the Centre while awaiting social services action. They wished to protect the child and do their best to ameliorate the situation in the interim. The NSO felt that trying to help and support the parents was also a duty to try to break the cycle of abuse but frontline staff felt that the potential harm to the child precluded this and the child was at risk if the situation was allowed to persist. The frontline staff felt disturbed that social services action was not immediate (there was previous history of abuse) and that their concerns regarding the strength of the case were not fully acknowledged, increasing the potential for harm. The NSO wondered if she had become inured to some extent from extensive experience and had not fully recognized the strength of evidence from the initial signs of neglect. The whole team felt vulnerable, frustrated and increasingly powerless and concerned for the child the longer the case went on. This created powerful emotional reactions which were not fully resolved when social services did take action.

The review found common perspectives on what went well: procedural compliance; building rapport with the family (enabling communication and continued attendance); a working environment that enabled open discussion and professional challenge at all levels in the team. The frontline practitioners found the supportive emotional containment provided by their line manager invaluable during the case. This couldn't, however, overcome the feeling of vulnerability from being left to 'hold' the situation while awaiting communication from social services or reduce the fear for the child.

The review produced some practical recommendations for practices which would heighten early recognition of concerns and substantiate evidence for assessing and reporting. These were incorporated into a revised safeguarding policy. There was also recognition of the emotional support strategies needed during such cases and ways to strengthen these. The review produced leadership learning in the team, recognizing the value of shared reflections and constructive challenge of practice from every level in the organization and the valid place of reason and emotion in that process. The NSO remarked later that: 'The review gave us permission to let go of negative emotions.'

This scenario illustrates why we need to utilize both emotion and reason in the reflective process. Feelings are engaged in our thought processes, holding contradictions and tensions which are part of the complex nature of human experience. The tensions felt in the team were born out of passionate care for children's well-being and the desire to contribute actively to that purpose. This common understanding gave the team the leadership impetus for self-review to learn from the experience. The diffusion of reflective integrity in this organization enabled the team to adopt both an individual and dialogic model of reflection examining the differential enactment of values in the situation, as well as to reconcile actions and feelings that were aroused in the process. The presence of trusting and open relationships enabled constructive challenge and engagement with each other's dispositions. This has parallels with 'relational agency' which Edwards and D'Arcy (2004) consider to be necessary for social learning and is part of *relational interdependence* in this community (see Chapters 6 and 9).

Argyris and Schön (1974) recognized that cognitive dissonance can emerge during the reflective process of 'double-loop learning', which lays bare underlying assumptions and norms of practice for examination. They consider it necessary to open up this uncomfortable space in order to provide scope for revising beliefs and changing practices, but they did not pursue the essential place of emotions in dealing with this. Rosenberg (2010), like Jordi (2011), calls for an integrative perspective, seeing reflective practice as contributing to human happiness, bringing body and soul together by giving feelings a place in the process. She argues that reflective practice enhances drive, purpose and focus and gives meaning to our actions, which is fundamental to human happiness: 'We feel connected to what is beyond our inner world through the positivity that we contribute to it' (Rosenberg 2010: 14). This helps to explain why passionate care for children's well-being and development motivates early years practitioners and prompts the desire to make a difference through actively working for the well-being of the child. Passionate care strengthens the resolve to tackle difficult professional issues and provides a dynamic for the affective element in reflective leadership practice. In Scenario 1, the frontline practitioners were exercising leadership by calling for a case review where they could share perspectives and collectively examine the uncomfortable space between their beliefs and actions (espoused theory and theory in action) through the process of reflective integrity.

This does not mean to suggest that universal agreement or simple solutions can be arrived at easily through shared professional reflection. Conflicting interests and perspectives take multiple forms, for example between providers and stakeholders, government policy and pedagogical principles and different disciplines in the sector. Added to this are the varied organizational, economic and social pressures which affect policy and practice, revealing the multiplicity of influences which could give rise to different ways of seeing any given situation. This is where dialogic models of reflection based on ethical principles and common purpose help to deal with value conflicts, as they require practitioners to seek to understand their own and others' points of view (Kinsella 2010). Such models also allow emotion to be expressed as part of the process of understanding. Reflective leadership practice then becomes less about solving problems and more about the way we navigate complex situations individually and collectively. When reflective integrity is diffused through an organization or group, difficult situations are not left to fester; instead it gives impetus and strategies to examine and address them, dealing with conflict constructively for the purpose of learning from experience.

Integrity: consistency and competency

Just as we are not taking a traditional view of reflection, neither do we adopt the simple interpretation of integrity as acting in accordance with an accepted ethical code or a given set of values. We are working with the idea of integrity as a more 'situationally related competence' (Edgar and Pattison 2011: 95) which enables practitioners to deal with the messy complexity of professional life where situations entail conflicting values and priorities and where dilemmas and tensions occur, as demonstrated in Scenario 1.

Consistency is generally seen as important in the simple view of integrity as it confirms an internal theory of self and provides predictability and trust-worthiness for others. In individualist cultures, actions are justified in terms of a personal view of moral correctness and ideals regarding professional behav-iour. If this internal view of professional self expects complete correlation between values and actions then it is likely to produce negative feelings of guilt or self-reproof when we find them out of alignment. Alternatively, it could lead to arrogant self-righteousness, believing there is only one way of doing things, or might equally apply to consistent action based on prejudice or harmful beliefs. Consistency in itself has no moral basis and there is no yard-stick to measure the degree or correctness of it. Critical reflective review, there-fore, is an essential element of integrity – otherwise the simple view could prevail, bringing a danger of holding steadfast to an inflexible set of beliefs. Where a more socially constructed view of self is applied, the individual is viewed within a social network, defined more by personal and group relation-ships and expectations (Cross *et al.* 2003). So when reflection is combined with integrity, thinking includes but goes beyond the individual to involve a re-appraisal of the norms and beliefs of practice as they operate in any given situ-ation, taking the perspectives of others into account. This creates openness to difference and change for individuals and organizations, and change is frequently the focus of leadership practice, as illustrated in Scenario 2.

Leadership scenario 2: Children's Centre Board of Trustees meeting

The Trustee Board provides the governance for the Children's Centre and is made up of volunteers from different professional backgrounds plus the Children's Centre Manager and Deputy. The board members have varied social, political and religious beliefs and individual reasons for being a trustee but all have a strong sense of community purpose and belief in the ethos of the Children's Centre. The Children's Centre has articulated values in its mission statement.

The Centre is going through a period of rapid change, with expansion of premises and core purpose at a time of shrinking funding streams. Economic sustainability has become a guiding principle and there has been a move to develop a business arm for income generation. Business experts among the trustees have led proposals for business development and reorganization of legal and management structures to install a Board of Directors and split the current and future functions of the Centre between income-generating and charitable purposes. At a Board meeting focusing on dividing up the Centre functions to correspond in this way, the Trustees with business expertise adopted an 'expert' and task-orientated approach to execute the task without inviting a broad discussion. Although no one expressed concerns at the time, the Centre managers felt uncertain and a little uneasy about the proposal. They felt that the overall charitable values and purpose of the Centre seemed threatened and in danger of being lost. They were concerned about how they could continue to present the organization as charitable for external promotion and felt that sponsorship could be affected. They were also concerned that the proposed split of staff between charity and business would be divisive and unwelcome and could potentially undermine staff commitment and motivation to work. Consequently, the managers shared their concerns and asked the Board to give the matter further consideration.

At the next meeting, the Chair of the Board gave opportunity for concerns to be voiced and the Board members were open to this feedback. In the ensuing discussion, the Trustees made specific reference to the importance of keeping to the Centre values in the way they worked and that decisions should not compromise the mission and values. This led to considering trustee interpretations of the Centre values when personal beliefs were voiced, both religious and secular, which supported their individual commitment. Whilst there were some strongly expressed differences between these underpinning beliefs and world-views, there was commonality in the consequent values derived from them. It was possible, therefore, to agree that the way the Board worked should reflect those values while recognizing the personal validity of different world-views which would most likely require continuing negotiation. The Chairperson posed a reflective question to the trustees, asking whether the Board in the previous meeting had enabled sufficient opportunity for different perspectives to be voiced, or had been receptive enough to listen.

Consequently, the Board revisited the basis of the decision in this light and checks and balances were built into the business charter to ensure that the business imperative did not act contrary to the charitable motivations and mission. A mechanism to assure this was incorporated into the legal arrangements for the business arm to guide potential decision-making dilemmas in the future. All staff members were placed under the charity and the subsidiary nature of the business to the charity was re-established.

Although misgivings were overlooked at the time of the meeting, the seeming incongruence between decisions and the Centre's values caused sufficient concern for a challenge to be raised. This suggests both an expectation and a strong desire to work in a way that produces some level of synergy between personal and organizational action and values. There was also an expectation that the Board would be receptive to seeing values embodied in the organizational mission fulfilled through policy, and therefore observable in practice. This provided the impetus not to let it lie but also invited potential conflict.

Mission and value statements tend to be aspirational and are embodied in policies as a means to translate these aspirations into practice. They are seen as a leadership tool. Nevertheless, this does not necessarily represent what actually happens. As Spillane *et al.* (2004:14) suggest, the gap between intentions, beliefs and actions 'can be maintained without duplicitous intent' because official policies tend not to be flexible enough to take into account the complexity and variety of circumstances that make up everyday practice. In retrospective examination, we tend to underplay the uncertainties and contradictions faced at the time, thus rationalizing events and actions. Daily practice becomes guided by 'theories in use', which can differ substantially from the 'espoused theory' that we claim guides our actions (Argyris and Schön 1974). This is where the process of reflective integrity becomes essential in two ways: it heightens awareness of this potential gap, prompting thinking on how to reduce it; and it opens up assumptions within the underlying value base to critical examination, enabling flexibility and potential compromise. This is why reflection and integrity need to work together to avoid the danger of dogmatism or idealism which does not sufficiently acknowledge the complex social nature of everyday life and work.

A didactic perspective of integrity is concerned with the simple 'rightness' of a moral principle which does not recognize the strength and success in being able to work with values relative to each situation. In Scenario 2, the Board adopted reflective integrity by going beyond the question, 'Are we being true to our values and purpose in our everyday actions and behaviour?' to engage in critical re-examination of those values in an operational context, considering alternative perspectives and bearing the situation and evidence in mind. The Trustees, as the governing body, had self-expectations to exemplify leadership in critically reflecting on their decisions and behaviour in relation to the Centre values. In this way, the Trustees exhibited integrity as 'reflective competence' which produces compromises that remain compatible with beliefs and values, working with and negotiating 'the bundle of personal, organizational, and professional values and ethos with which [we] are confronted' (Edgar and Pattison 2011: 98). This allows for a more human and pragmatic expectation of behaviour and recognizes the complex nature of practice. There may be a danger, however, of appearing always to seek the middle ground, which could end up avoiding challenge or producing an outcome that suits no one or the situation. Nevertheless, it does remind us that, in organizational life, no one is likely to be able to act without affecting others and taking intransigent personal beliefs as the basis for practice is more likely to lead to conflict than harmony.

The expectation of total synergy between beliefs and practices is therefore no measure for integrity as it is unrealistic, uncompromising and does not reflect the complexity or diversity of human nature or the world of work. There is a need to take others and their world-views into account, so there is bound to be some compromise. What matters, however, is not what compromise is reached or who has the greatest conscience but how you get there and the process undertaken.

> Integrity is not so much an authoritative and fixed aspect of the self that must be respected and obeyed no matter what. It is a more deliberate capacity and competence which is deployed in the context of complex professional and organizational work to find appropriate answers and ways forward.
>
> (Edgar and Pattison 2011: 103)

Viewed in this way, integrity becomes a social competence presupposing membership of a community with responsibilities to others. Sergiovanni (1998) emphasizes the need for educational leadership to be based on communities of responsibility in order to build leadership 'capital'. So the idea of integrity as a social competence could be considered an integral element of building leadership as a form of human capital. Viewed as a competence, integrity is not fixed but can be nurtured and developed. Dweck (2008) argues that 'malleable intelligence' can be taught, developing theories of self which make us more eager to learn, to seek challenge and be self-regulating. For this to happen, much depends on the experience and expectations of positive messages and responses from others in our daily interactions and relationships. Edgar and Pattison (2011: 100) suggest that

> [t]he main exemplars of integrity are people who can skilfully identify and navigate the sorts of compromises that are inevitable in complex work in pluriform social contexts where your own personal values, however precious to yourself, are regarded as only part of the relevant picture.

A leadership-rich organization which practises reflective integrity supports positive relationships by removing the anxiety of uncertain or negative responses to a situation. This removes the fear of undermining core beliefs and theories of self which lead to defensiveness rather than openness. Reflective integrity therefore enables engagement with the value position of others with the understanding that is important in order for trusting relationships to develop. Scenario 2 showed how the Trustees were willing to listen and take a collective approach to honest appraisal of their actions and decisions while also considering the frame in which others viewed the decisions (Kinsella 2010).The decision-making process was reviewed with reference to personal belief systems and their relationship to individual commitment to the Centre's values and mission. These stemmed from strongly held but conflicting world-views which produced tensions that might have been debilitating to the trustee leadership of the Centre. There were also conflicting tensions between chari-table and business drivers which could occur again in the future. There was a need, therefore, to find negotiated solutions which would permit compromise without undermining either individual or organizational values and without losing sight of the essential nature and purpose of the organizational mission. To do this requires critical, creative and emotional engagement with the people, the organization and the factors relevant to any situation in order to mediate commonalities and differences.

Edgar and Pattison (2011: 95) suggest that integrity 'can most usefully be seen as a competence or capacity for reflection and discernment in the midst of the conflicting demands between professional and personal values, roles and ethical systems'. They recognize, however, that it is strongly associated with interpersonal relations and organizational behaviour and suggest, 'It is within the strain and conflict between personal and professional values, including organizational values, that integrity becomes an important concept' (Edgar and Pattison 2011: 97).

Integrating reflection and integrity

By bringing the concepts of reflection and integrity together in the term reflec-tive integrity we make clear that they are integral to each other and directly linked to leadership through change and learning. Reflective integrity is a process of examining the complex ambiguities and contradictions which arise in everyday pedagogical and leadership practice in order to consider the effi-cacy of action or potential action. Reflection raises integrity above simple assertion of a moral principle to prevent complacency developing. The process of reflective integrity can produce new or revised thinking which prompts action to change and incorporate different behaviour into daily practice. It forms part of leadership by enhancing the capacity to learn and change for the principal purpose of making things better and creating a positive difference. Rosenberg (2010: 11) suggests that 'this notion of leadership pertains not only to those who have leadership titles; it applies to each and every human being', and argues that we all have the capacity and capability to contribute to change by changing ourselves through reflective practice. If we recognize that self-change has an influence on other events and people with whom we have an association, then we contribute to change which can be organizational and systemic; we need to take responsibility for that and embrace our ability to make a difference. This is where catalytic agency and reflective integrity have a symbiotic relationship, integrating purposeful drive, reflection and integrity, so that we act meaningfully and learn through adaptation and change for a common purpose.

Combining reflection with integrity brings mind and heart together to prevent purely rational or emotional positioning to justify actions, behaviour and decisions and to avoid unexamined reliance on values, beliefs and practices. Reflective integrity recognizes the emotional challenge implicit in examining beliefs and opens up potential for positive utilization of the affective domain to prompt and review actions for meaningful change. It is a developmental process, more productive and flexible, more forgiving, tolerant and attainable and more constructive than either concept alone.

The process of reflective integrity can be applied in the diffused dimension of leadership to examine tensions, anxiety or unresolved emotional concerns related to work and the enactment of values at work. Organizations require a learning orientation which prompts collective examination beyond the surface of events or actions in order to learn. Reflective integrity reviews the reliability of tacit knowledge, to check that it holds good or whether revision is necessary in the light of new experience or learning. It utilizes cognition and emotion in this process. Undertaking reflective integrity highlights disparity between beliefs, values and actions. It does this, not as a judgement or measure, but to prompt behaviour to challenge, reassess and negotiate validity in different circumstances, taking into account a range of world-views. Reflective integrity is characteristic of *leadership within* where leadership is a participative process through which the organizational community collectively attends to a common purpose.

Reflective prompts

1   What view of reflection informs your practice? What do you consider to be the pros and cons of acknowledging and using emotion as part of the reflective process?

2   If integrity can be viewed as a social competency, how can it be developed through professional training? How would this support leadership development?

3   What aspects of this chapter enable you to consider how you could practise reflective integrity with others, whatever position you hold in the organization?

9 Relational interdependence: diffusing leadership in community

> All the higher functions originate as actual relations between human individuals.
>
> (*Vygotsky, Mind in Society: The Development of Higher Psychological Processes*)

Vygotsky considered learning as one of the higher human functions, placing the learning of culture and concepts within a process of human interaction (Vygotsky 1978:57). He argues that culture and ideas are mediated socially and then become internalized and accommodated in our individual thinking. Leadership plays a significant part in the development and transmission of culture through the medium of relationships in the social environment of work. Leading and learning become interconnected as part of the human drive to know and make sense of the world so that we can act purposefully in it. 'The innate desire for meaning contributes to internal change efforts' (Rosenberg 2010: 12) and the desire to act with purpose is a central element of leadership. We consider, therefore, that both leadership and learning are part of the higher functions of human society because they are located in reciprocal and interdependent relationships. This is why relational interdependence features prominently in the paradigm of *leadership within*.

The close connection between leadership and learning through the concept of transformation has been well developed, particularly in the idea of the learning community (Senge 1993; Argyris and Schön 1996). Both leadership and learning are a form of social practice acted out through participation and in relationship to others. Lave and Wenger (1996: 145) argue that 'social practice emphasizes the relational interdependency of agent and world, activity, meaning, cognition, learning and knowing.' It is the interconnectedness of individuals and their social world and the significance of constructive relationships and mutual dependency that we wish to demonstrate through relational interdependence as a valuable element of leadership.

The paradigm of *leadership within* recognizes the essentially relational and interdependent nature of human society. Whilst we incorporate a notion of self-leadership, recognizing individual agency and self-responsibility which we have called *inner* leadership, this is balanced by a more social, participative and inclusive understanding of leadership as a human phenomenon which operates within and across groups and organizations. When leadership is *diffused* in this way it can create a 'leadership-rich' learning community.

Building community

It is a natural human desire to seek purpose in our lives and derive meaning from our experiences in order to validate who we are (Rogers 1983). Self-validation has a relational aspect to others with whom we live and work (Billett 2006, 2008) and therefore a sense of being valued and valuing others is critical in building a positive community identity. Relational interdependence enables internalization of a culture which values the strengths and differences of each person and increases the sense of self-worth in the individual. This means that nurturing and maintaining constructive and inclusive relationships is an essential part of the social practice of leadership in order to enhance a sense of personal value, belonging and participation in a worthwhile endeavour. Sergiovanni (2001: 61) views community as 'a moral phenomenon rather than simply a geographic or territorial entity' which provides a sense of belonging and identity, where leadership is based on enacting values and beliefs and realizing hopes and dreams. A web of meaningful relationships develops around a common focus or mutual interest which creates a sense of purpose, encouraging a desire to participate and contribute in some way. Relational interdependence encourages this response, sometimes as a return on the emotional investment that has been shown through acceptance and support in the community.

In ECEC, leadership is pedagogical in nature because the prime concern is to promote the education and well-being of young children and their families which involves the whole environment of the child and is therefore a broad community with a common interest and responsibility. Speaking in the context of school leadership, Sergiovanni (1998: 37) suggests that '[t]o understand pedagogical leadership one must understand the story of community', arguing that value is added to children's learning through building human capital in the whole school community. This is demonstrated in non-school settings in the examples in Chapter 6 where June's pedagogical leadership is based on the involvement and reciprocal relationships of staff and community. The stock of human capital is increased by working together as a community, creating shared concern for the best outcomes for children and families. This encourages an understanding of the need to share effective practice in the professional community and beyond, acknowledging and drawing on the strengths, expertise and creative capabilities of individuals and groups regardless of position or role. It recognizes the relational interdependence of human beings in creating common purpose and building human and social capital.

While Sergiovanni (1998) uses the contemporary terminology of leaders and followers, we argue that this is unhelpful when pursuing ideas of community responsibility and participative concepts of leadership. Leadership engagement goes far beyond this to involve the whole community in a more diffused way, which obviates the need to make distinctions between leaders and followers. Nevertheless, Sergiovanni (1998: 41) contributes a powerful idea of leadership, which is that the community that reflects together learns, inquires and cares together, 'constructing a reality that helps them to navigate through a complex world'. This is demonstrated in the following personal reflections of two long-standing Family Centre users.

Learning journeys

This is the story of two women, known here as Brenda and Anne, who recorded their relationship and involvement with a Family Centre through the medium of an 'altered book'. This was a form of scrapbook in which they placed reflective accounts, selected episodes and artefacts to record their interpretation of their personal journey of development from the time they first attended the Family Centre. This was part of a life-story approach to collecting evidence (Creswell 2009) for a narrative research project related to Family Centre impact from the viewpoint of its users. Ethical procedures for educational research were followed (BERA 2004) and permissions sought from the Centre and the participants for extracts from the data to be used in this way.

When they first came into contact with the Centre, Brenda and Anne each had a young baby and were new to the area. They felt isolated and in need of some social contact and occasional relief from parenting. Over a period of six years their involvement with the Centre grew. Initially they used the Centre for services such as mother and baby groups and for crèche facilities, giving them 'time out' to undertake courses. They went on to participate in family days, fundraising and eventually to work with the Centre to set up a business selling craft items made by themselves and other members of the Centre community. They built up a strong connection to each other and the Centre which they credited for inspiring them with self-belief, encouragement and opportunities which transformed their lives. Their stories reveal the relational interdependence of the Centre community where human capital is developed incrementally and mutual gains are made, encouraged by a fundamental belief in human potential to develop and make meaningful use of individual skills and abilities. In developing themselves, Brenda and Anne not only gained personally but contributed to the purpose, practice and development of the organization in what we would term a diffused leadership process.

For Brenda and Anne, the process of creating the scrapbook was an aid to reflection and revealed increasing awareness of the significant role the Centre plays in their lives.

> Until I did the book I had no idea what a part of my life they [the Centre community] really are. They have done so much for me and whatever the future holds I hope I stay connected here.
>
> (Brenda)

Anne also feels strongly connected:

> You could say it was the end of my time with the Centre as I started coming here when my daughter was nine months old and then with my son and now he has started school. So, going forward, my involvement with the Centre is going to be on a more personal level. I'd like to give back to them. I don't see it ending really.

These interview extracts show the strength of identity with and commitment to the Centre community which is creating a desire to reciprocate the benefit they feel they have gained. Brenda refers to the Centre as a 'family' in her scrapbook (Figure 9.1). The use of the term 'family' is no coincidence, not only because the Centre is called a Family Centre and has families as its focus but because it operates with the ethos of a family, nurturing potential and being concerned for the well-being of all those involved or connected to it. This is an intentional way of working to create a community which incorporates staff, governors, users and all who come into contact with the Centre. The analogy is apt as the Family Centre provides a sense of safety in an environment which is non-judgemental and where individuals feel intrinsically valued, supported and protected. In this way the Centre nurtures the nutrients for human growth within the community, enabling personal development and movement from dependency to independence. Yet Brenda and Anne, along with other Centre users, remain connected to the Centre through relational interdependence combined with a sense of unconditional regard (Rogers 1961) which supports self-validation and self-belief, strengthening the identity that comes from belonging to a community.

Releasing human potential

Both Brenda and Anne tend to view themselves as recipients, gaining from what the Centre has done for them, particularly in gaining confidence and self-belief (Figure 9.2):

Figure 9.1   The Centre family

> The Centre has given me the opportunities to grow. It was quite a big step for me to go initially. I find it challenging to walk into a new place but now, the whole knowing who I am, building my personality, making friends, meeting people – that's how I've gained through coming here.
>
> (Anne)

What Anne and Brenda recognize as significant is the belief and encouragement shown in them by the Centre staff which bolstered their self-confidence and spurred them to take risks and challenge themselves. Taking risks is a key leadership challenge and the relational trust built up through their interactions with the Centre staff released their potential (see Figure 9.3).

> Doing all the courses is something I never imagined. When I gave up work to have kids I had no idea that I would learn these skills and do

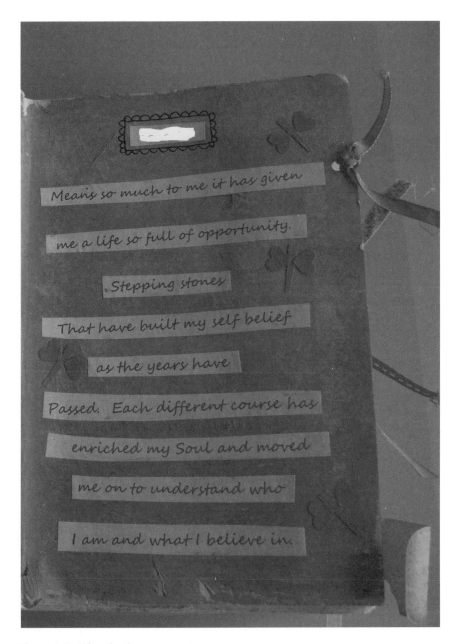

Figure 9.2 What the Centre means to me

Figure 9.3 Learning together

> things like web design. I have launched a business and run a shop and
> that wouldn't have happened had it not been for the Centre.
>
> (Brenda)

Brenda and Anne felt that their personal and creative talent was released as a result of encouragement to attend courses at the Centre which went beyond their estimate of their own ability (Figure 9.3). Their achievements on these courses, their certificates and qualifications, incrementally increased their self-belief to go further. The belief the Centre staff had in them and the way they valued their creative flair helped them to see further opportunities for themselves in selling their craft items. As they went through their stories, Brenda and Anne recognized that this has been a reciprocal process of learning and achievement between them and the Centre staff and community. Brenda and Anne now run a shop selling their own creative artefacts and those of other Centre users which contributes a small economic return to the Centre as well. Consequently they realize that they are setting an example and being a role model for others by their business presence in the community and also by sharing their journey, showing what it is possible to achieve. They are, as Sergiovanni (1998) suggests, exercising leadership by learning, reflecting and caring together and this is taken forward into mutually beneficial action supported by a relationally interdependent community.

> By setting up the shop we have helped quite a lot of people realize their
> talents. We have given a lot of people confidence in their creative belief.
> We've just given them the opportunity as well.
>
> (Anne)

Individual and social agency both play a part in constructing identity and meaning for individuals and groups in the workplace: 'Creativity is unleashed within people when they are given leadership opportunities to pursue issues related to their personal passions and concerns' (Slater 2008: 59). This influences others in the community, creating norms of active participation and increasing the stock of human and social capital. Appreciation of the relational interdependence of children, parents, professionals and agencies releases human assets in pursuit of common goals, creating the opportunity for an open and inclusive concept of leadership. Lambert (2003) considers leadership to be a reciprocal process enabling all members of the community to play a part in constructing meaning which leads to common purposes. This breaks down barriers created by thinking of leadership as the prerogative of the few and enables more broad-based participation and contribution, enhancing community learning and creating leadership capital. Greater leadership capital provides sustainability and a generative form of leadership which may require a level of continuity to establish the culture and practices but does not come and go with a single individual.

The social and cultural situation of the setting produces common under-standing and norms of behaviour and practice, so that even when a person appears to be acting alone, he or she is carrying 'cultural baggage' which can either release or constrain agency. Leadership practices help to create but are also affected by the socio-cultural situation (Spillane *et al.* 2004), which is why an inclusive, relationally interdependent notion of leadership is receptive to and encourages diverse participation, to release rather than constrain poten-tial. The relational interdependence of social and personal agency in working practices needs greater recognition in order to understand how individuals are active participants in making and transforming culture (Billett 2008).

Valuing others

Relational interdependence acknowledges individual strengths and the strength derived from collective endeavour. It can be manifested in separate individuals working in parallel for the same end; as joint actors working together utilizing respective strengths; or as a community of diverse elements working sometimes together and sometimes separately to complement each other and therefore create a greater combined strength. Overall it builds collective responsibility and shared leadership. As indicated in Chapter 6, the specific focus of activity is not in itself the issue but the process of working in a relationally interdependent manner. Working in this way respects, engages and invites participation, leading to successful utilization of talent and creating opportunities for innovation and change. This form of leadership invites all those connected to the organization to become social actors in making sense of and shaping their environment.

When relational interdependence is fostered throughout an organization, leadership becomes diffused and pervasive, occurring in every quarter, taking many different forms. The many forms of leadership involvement come from valuing the diverse skills and talents of its staff and community and their potential to learn and contribute to the overall development of the group. The personal stories of Brenda and Anne show service users becoming engaged in and contributing to leadership.

> The shop is away from the children and it started when they went to school – when my ties with the Family Centre would have gone! We did it all; we painted it, got the furniture, we do the banking. We get to sell our work in return and people see what we do. It means the town knows who we are and what we do.
>
> (Anne)

There is a conflation of identity here in the use of 'we', meaning both Brenda and Anne and the Family Centre. Yet, while Brenda and Anne see themselves as part of the Centre community, they may not recognize themselves as engaging in leadership. This is where traditional views of leadership are limiting but there is no doubting that Brenda and Anne are making a leadership contribution to the Centre and its community. They represent the Centre in the community through their shop; they are role models for other service users; they contribute to the vision and mission by presenting their work (and by implication their achievements) literally in the shop front, promoting community involvement. There is mutual dependency and benefit for Brenda, Anne and the Centre, showing the essential place of reciprocal and interdependent relationships. Brenda and Anne, like staff and other users, were encouraged by the belief shown in them and the valuing of their abilities and developing skills. Brenda and Anne were further motivated to pursue higher goals by the friendship of other service users and because of the successes and achievements they experienced which went beyond their expectations. The opportunity to use their skills, for example by leading workshops, further enhanced their self-belief and demonstrated that they had skills to offer back to the community (Figure 9.4).

The idea of relational interdependence does not underplay individual capacity to act but recognizes and releases potential for everyone to contribute

Figure 9.4   Reciprocal skill development

by starting from a perspective of valuing others. It encourages development of the capacity to engage with the disposition of others, described by Edwards and D'Arcy (2004) as 'relational agency', which they suggest is a significant process in the social aspect of learning. Leadership and learning as social practices require the ability to engage with the disposition of others in order to build effective relationships which can release human potential. This is particularly apt for ECEC where, in its nature, learning and the world of work are essentially intertwined. Vygotsky (1978) saw learning as interactive and interrelational where the connectivity between individuals supports sense-making. Similarly, in the context of work, the capacity to recognize and use each other as a resource enhances our interpretation of a situation and the ability to deal with a problem or practice. Relational interdependence thus supports individual as well as collective learning and action. It is this interplay between personal and social agency which creates conditions for constructive leadership processes which inevitably involve some reciprocity or mutual benefit. The process of relational interdependency diffused in a leadership-rich community can have profound effects on the lives of its community members, as illustrated in the personal stories presented in this chapter.

Vygotsky (1978) suggested that transformation occurs when external activity is reconstructed internally. The moral valuing of others which occurs in the social practice of leadership, as shown in these learning journeys, turns belief shown by others into self-belief and supports success spurring further achievement (Rogers 1961). The connectivity to others developed in this way reinforces relational interdependence in a constructive cycle of trusting relationships and through identity with the community in common purpose.

Trust

The relational interdependence between personal growth and development of the Centre community members is mirrored in the mission of the Centre itself and is exhibited in the relationships and identity built up as part of that community. Kaser and Halbert's (2009) concept of 'relational trust' as a leadership mindset offers another view on the significance of interdependent relationships. Whilst they tend to focus on individuals as leaders, though not exclusively principals, they see the invested leader's mindset as crucial in building culture and setting the leadership model. They argue for building trust, shown through caring, as a necessary ingredient of positive relationships. This means going beyond the minimum by showing sensitivity, personal interest, knowledge of individual circumstances, working with others' strengths and interests, being non-judgemental, listening and supporting others to find their own solutions. There are parallels here with 'relational agency' (Edwards and D'Arcy 2004), which is engaging with the disposition of others and a willingness to understand other perspectives, showing mutual respect and regard to generate confident relationships in which people can flourish and learn. This provides sufficient trust to share concerns and uncertainties in order to learn: 'In the positive school communities we have observed, respect is generally based on the belief of all individuals that they are being deeply listened to and understood, rather than just being heard' (Kaser and Halbert 2009: 50).

Relational interdependence requires trust which is founded on a shared faith in the benevolence and concern for well-being in the group. It requires demonstration of belief in human potential and capability. It celebrates success. Building trust in a community reduces negativity and disabling emotions which inhibit growth, development and learning. Trust encourages risk-taking to try new things. Kaser and Halbert (2009) argue that trusting relationships build positive cultures and are part of daily routines and interactions. They build the confidence needed for new practices by moderating stress, risk and feelings of vulnerability. Trusting cultures provide inner and corporate strength to choose what path to follow and help resist conformity to conflicting external demands (Kaser and Halbert 2009). Such challenges are frequently posed for ECEC communities and trust can be easily lost if difficult situations or conflicting demands are not addressed. Yet challenging situations become burdensome if expectations to address and resolve them lie in the nominated lead person alone because of traditional concepts of leadership. By fostering relational interdependence in community, shared responsibility is assumed for examining, addressing, negotiating and mediating conflict. The expectation of always needing to resolve conflict can tend to push differences below the surface but where complexity in human relations is acknowledged and multiple perspectives are seen as a strength they are more likely to be voiced and therefore available for greater understanding and consideration. Conflict can then be turned into healthy debate and constructive challenge, especially when founded on a common experience of being valued and working for an ultimately worthwhile cause.

Working and caring together

Relational interdependence provides a trusting base for collaboration, communication, interaction, partnership and teamwork. These are particularly important aspects for multiagency, interdisciplinary work which features significantly in the ECEC sector in providing a holistic service for children and families. Aubrey (2011) describes children's centres as 'service hubs' engaging an array of professionals and disciplines in the delivery of services. This requires skills in boundary spanning and can create tensions and stress where professional identities, values and practices appear to be under threat. The challenge is to create ways of working which open up the potential for conflict and differences to be aired constructively and collectively examined, finding areas of commonality and acceptable compromise or accepting difference, without losing sight of the common purpose in working for the well-being of children and families. Working consciously to develop mutual trust and knowledge of each other's professional ethic will help to build confident interprofessional practice. The development of such knowledge and trust takes place through daily interactions, which is why relational interdependence offers great strength in developing interprofessional practice. Relational interdependence seeks to use and interweave each other's strengths into the whole of practice. Dialogue helps us to learn about each other, opening up opportunities for respectful and healthy discussion. Nevertheless it is important not to ignore conflict but seek to turn it into constructive challenge, prompting reflective integrity as a social competence to help understand and mediate differences together. As relational interdependence is founded on valuing difference it encourages engagement in this leadership process regardless of differences in status and professions. As Aubrey (2011) indicates, working towards a shared philosophy, vision, identity and purpose and developing common principles of practice is no easy task. Yet it is too important to leave to single individuals with the nominated role to lead, so rather than talking of leading multidisciplinary teams, which focuses on the person leading, we prefer to discuss leadership within those teams and communities in order to recognize the relational nature of the work. 'In contrast to traditional hierarchical and individualized approaches to leadership, shared leadership is dependent upon the professional norms of collaboration that rely on trust, respect for the expertise of others and mutual interdependence for success' (Slater 2008: 59). Payne (2000) suggests that not only will families get a better deal if we work together but we will also gain a safer and more worthwhile form of practice. Relational interdependence can be fostered through inclusive teamwork and open networks which provide the means to move away from the idea of leading as something other people do and recognize the leadership which takes place in community. We advocate shifting to a more participative concept of leadership which draws people in through relational interdependence.

Sergiovanni (1998: 43) suggests that: 'the source of authority for leadership is found neither in bureaucratic rules and procedures nor in the personalities and styles of leaders but in shared values, ideas and commitments.' This requires letting go of individualistic notions of power and the need to claim personal ownership of ideas in order to recognize the collective endeavour which requires working with complementary strengths and respect rather than measuring individual input or impact. There is greater advantage and therefore greater impact in working with collective strengths because the whole is significantly more than the sum of its parts.

Reflective prompts

1   Make a diagram/flowchart of current dependencies or interrelationships in a group context or setting in which you are involved. Who is dependent on whom for what? Include what you see as the main strengths or expertise, where they are located and how they contribute to the group purpose.
2   Now highlight the positive aspects and consider the relationship with the less positive aspects. How does this affect your view of relationships and the potential impact ultimately for children and families?
3   How can you draw in the potential for further or improved interdependence through constructive relationships? What further capacity could this achieve and what is needed to make it happen?

PART III
Developing leadership

10 *Leadership within*: a framework for development

We have argued throughout this book for a new paradigm of leadership which is more expansive and inclusive than currently prevailing concepts. In order to break down traditional thinking about leadership, we wish to take the 'leader' out of 'leadership' as an exercise to divert the focus from the person to the process, to disassociate leadership from management and to move away from viewing leadership as the province of the few who are at the top of the hierarchy. In the 1990s Senge (1993: 340) suggested that: 'at its heart, the traditional view of leadership is based on assumptions of people's powerlessness, their lack of personal vision and inability to master the forces of change, deficits which can be remedied only by a few great leaders.' We wish to counter the disabling consequences of such traditional views of leadership which still prevail and which are too limited and limiting in scope to reflect the essential nature of ECEC. We are seeking new ways of conceptualizing leadership which liberate a broader community to participate more knowingly in leadership, thereby developing human potential, increasing leadership capacity and expanding the stock of social capital. Reliance on traditional ideologies of leadership has provided ill-fitting models for ECEC, which have not been derived from the sector, and leave a rather unsatisfactory and insufficiently flexible perspective on which to move forward. The development of the EYP as a pedagogical leader sits awkwardly with traditional notions of leadership as the leadership it requires needs to be capable of being exercised without invested position, power or management responsibility; this requires new thinking about leadership which breaks down hierarchical boundaries. We believe the idea of 'leading from within' can be better realized if the notion is based on leadership processes rather than individual competencies or tasks, on the purpose rather than the role, and sees leadership and learning as arising from 'within' the professional community. A paradigm shift which derives from the sector and better reflects the essential nature of early years could give confidence and opportunity to create greater leadership capacity and broader involvement in the central leadership purpose of improving children's learning and well-being.

Ebbeck and Waniganayake (2003) argue for opening up opportunities for practitioners to release their leadership potential. An obstacle to this is that while practitioners commonly attribute their motivation and professionalism to a desire to improve the education and well-being of children and their families, they rarely see themselves as fulfilling that through engaging in leadership. Speaking in the school context, Lambert (2003) argues that leadership is the right and responsibility of all teachers and that they have the capability to engage in leadership if the context is conducive. Leadership development in ECEC might also benefit from paying attention to creating a context in which leadership responsibility and capability is recognized and allowed to flourish as part of professionalism. By taking the 'leader' emphasis out of 'leadership' it no longer lies in the domain of the few but becomes something we can all engage in, raising confidence, utilizing skills and expertise and encouraging mutual responsibility. We have applied and extended these ideas to embrace the whole community of early years settings: families, staff, managers, associated professionals, broadening the notion of leadership to a process of action and interaction which is based on a common desire to promote well-being and development. This deliberately moves the spotlight away from the personhood of the leader which has dominated leadership literature and public perception because of the reliance it places on individual dispositions and skills and which does not generate or promote sustainability. In proposing the paradigm of *leadership within,* we are raising the possibility of an inclusive and participatory perspective. This acknowledges and values the diverse ways in which people can contribute to the process of leadership, fulfilling the fundamental human desire to create meaning and purpose for themselves.

We agree with Lambert (2003: 423) that 'we must depart from the familiar if we are to redefine leadership for the new century.' As most previous educational leadership research and literature has focused on positional leaders, largely school head teachers, the search for understanding has continued to be confined to examining the personality, skills, actions or behaviour of the nominated lead person and a division has been drawn between leaders and followers. This alienates others who do not see themselves included or represented in the required leader skill set. In moving away from the familiar we have sought illustrative evidence of engagement in leadership from a broad spectrum of frontline practitioners, parents, governors (trustees), as well as managers in a range of non-school settings. This supports a reconceptualization of leadership which is more likely to be relevant to the ECEC sector. We have drawn attention to relationships, interaction, agency, values and reflective activity in the three features of *leadership within to* complement the essence of early years pedagogy and professionalism. Leadership then becomes a reciprocal process of sense-making and shared purpose in which learning is integral. Whilst we have not drawn on school settings to illustrate our paradigm this does not mean to exclude the application of the paradigm in that context. We have drawn on school leadership literature but as this is predominantly based on those in nominated lead roles we felt it was important to give voice to less well-represented elements in ECEC. Nevertheless, we hope that the underpinning basis of the paradigm in the common leadership purpose and pedagogy of early years has something to offer the school-based early years community.

Leadership within – paradigm summary

We have portrayed the paradigm of *leadership within* operating in two dimensions:

Inner leadership, which relates to personal self- management, motivation, practice, values and beliefs which affect individual behaviour, and **diffused leadership**, which relates to collective engagement in the purpose, values and practices of a community, group or organization.

This is a technical separation to aid examination and understanding of both the subjective, internal manifestation of leadership and the presence of relational leadership in organizational interaction. The individual, however, is not a contained entity operating in isolation but forms part of the environment and a wider system of relations which exert a reciprocal influence. These domains are, therefore, essentially interconnected and we have attempted to show this through illustrating the three features of the paradigm (catalytic agency, reflective integrity and relational interdependence) in both dimensions, in Chapters 4–9. This is illustrated diagrammatically in Figure 10.1.

Leadership within can apply to all aspects of early years leadership, whether pedagogical or organizational, individual or collective. The aspect of leadership under consideration at any given time may provide a different focus or emphasis, depending on whether the spotlight is on pedagogical or organizational matters. The distinctions may be helpful to demonstrate this but it should be noted that these are somewhat arbitrary and intended for elucidation, not a strict division in real life (Figure 10.2). In ECEC, the organizational and pedagogical mission is fundamentally the same – i.e. to further the moral purpose of enhancing learning and well-being. In this way leadership is everyone's concern – governors, managers, practitioners, staff, external professionals and agencies, parents, families and children. We have intentionally reflected this, as far as possible but not exhaustively, in our choice of research extracts illustrating leadership scenarios in Chapters 4–9.

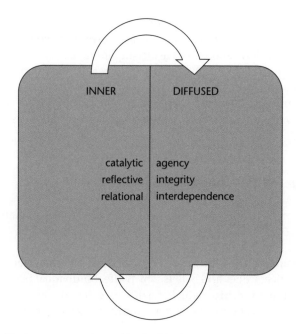

INNER	DIFFUSED
catalytic	agency
reflective	integrity
relational	interdependence

Figure 10.1   The interconnectedness of leadership domains

Leadership and learning

The relationship between leadership and learning has been well noted by researchers in the different domains of business, education and public service, including ECEC. Waniganayake (2002: 124) remarks that 'leading and learning go hand in hand', and this is particularly pertinent for organizations, such as early years settings, with learning as their core purpose. The idea of the learning organization (Argyris and Schön 1996) and learning communities makes leadership a shared responsibility which builds leadership capacity and participation through a shift in thinking and adaptation.

The link between leadership and learning is undisputed, whether couched in terms of individual or community development. Lambert (2003: 423) suggests that 'to be human is to learn, and to learn is to construct meaning and knowledge about the world that enables us to act purposefully.' In acting purposefully, we work together in leadership. We do this through interaction, dialogue and reflection, influencing each other in reciprocal relationships which draw people into the process of leadership. This is represented in Figure 10.3 as cogs interconnecting and propelling action and reaction.

Lambert (2003: 423) suggests that 'When actively engaged in reflective dialogue, adults become more complex in their thinking about the world,

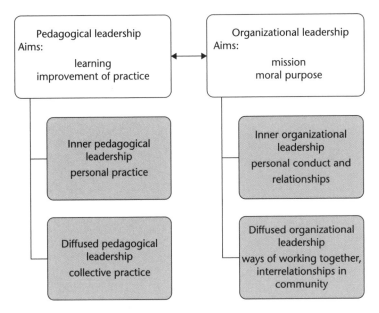

- Inner pedagogical leadership is focused on the self and personal practice; diffused pedagogical leadership is concerned with a collective approach to developing practice; and both have a common concern with learning.

- Inner organizational leadership is focused on personal workplace behaviour, conduct and relationships with others. Diffused organizational leadership is concerned with ways of working together and interrelationships in a community. Both are concerned to further the organizational aims and mission.

Figure 10.2   Comparison between pedagogical and organizational aspects of leadership

more respectful of diverse perspectives, more flexible and open toward new experiences.' This enables growth and learning to occur. Reflective dialogue is the basis for reflective integrity, illustrated in Chapters 5 and 8, paving the way for personal and collective learning through experience. This takes place in a community which acknowledges that we need to engage with each other in a relationally interdependent manner which values difference, works with strengths and actively engages with each other's perspectives. Leadership then becomes more inclusive when understood as the enactment of reciprocal and purposeful learning in the community (Sergiovanni 1998; Lambert 2003).

Leadership and learning are therefore both cultural and dialogic activities which create a form of social practice. They are each concerned with generating knowledge and change. The symbiotic relationship of learning,

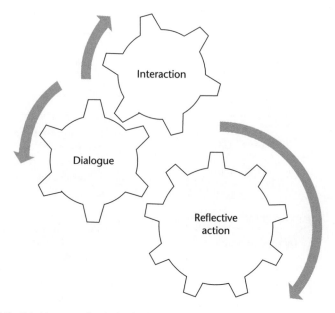

Figure 10.3 Working together in leadership

transformation and change (Lave and Wenger 1996) then creates a continuous cycle of constituting and reconstituting practice, whether organizational or pedagogical, in a process of catalytic agency.

If we are to break down conventional ideas of leadership then we may also break down similarly conventional ideas about leadership learning. Just as leadership has diverse meanings and interpretations, so does learning. Hager (2004) suggests that learning in the context of the workplace is not well understood and is predominantly seen as a product which is exhibited in individual competencies to be acquired, transferred and applied. This assumes that practice and the associated skills and competencies required are stable and can work in isolation, yet we know that practice is complex, social and ever-changing. Organizational and pedagogical practice is not simply the application of theory but an ongoing process of change, interaction, reflection and readjustment. A new paradigm of leadership, therefore, requires a new look at leadership learning and this has implications for the approach to leadership training and development.

Leadership training and development

Despite the increased focus on early years leadership over the past decade, Rodd suggests that it 'continues to be an enigma to many early childhood practitioners' (2006: 5). Aubrey draws attention to the relative absence of leadership development (2011) despite calls to plug the gap for those whose leadership training needs are unmet (Siraj-Blatchford and Manni 2007). Muijs *et al.* (2004) warn that lack of appropriate training means that nominated leaders might be significantly under-prepared for their roles. Official response to such concerns was evident in the creation of professional qualifications and status through NPQICL and EYPS (considered in Chapter 2). Increasingly complex demands on children's centres gave impetus to the development of NPQICL, intended to equip their nominated leaders with the necessary resilient behaviours, skills and understanding of interprofessional practice to fulfil their role. The view that leadership training is something to be offered to those in positions of authority or practitioners who aspire to such roles suggests that leadership training is viewed as individual, additional and supplementary rather than integral to professionalism. Aubrey (2011) argued that preparation for leadership should be available to all early childhood staff to promote sharing expertise and empowering collective agency for change. In addition, the expectation of pedagogical leadership entrusted to EYPs who do not necessarily hold posts of authority through which to bring about change raises further questions about preparation for leadership and who might demonstrate leadership practice (McDowall Clark and Baylis 2011; McDowall Clark in press). It is notable that none of the practitioners whose leadership profiles have been explored in the previous chapters has undertaken specific leadership training and yet their impact on practice is significant. Waniganayake (2002) has challenged the notion that leadership is a high order skill only to be practised by those already in positions of authority and we would support her view, suggesting that the concepts of leadership which underpin such a perspective are narrow and restrictive. Instead, we advocate opening up leadership by integrating it in the methods and approaches of the workplace and in initial professional training and continuing development.

Concepts of leadership patently affect the type and nature of any training or development which is available. Because of the conflation of leadership with management, training is frequently pragmatic and organizational with an emphasis on increasing the management skills of individuals (Muijs *et al.* 2004). Even when leader training is strategic or behavioural it still rests on the idea of power emanating from the top with one person or a few individuals having the greatest influence or holding the reins, although they might delegate some responsibility to others. Our paradigm requires a very different form of training and capacity building which avoids too much emphasis on the individual as a leader, to focus instead on the ability of everyone to practise leadership. Day (2001) also points out how the majority of investment and training is intended to develop individual leadership for those in formal authority roles rather than create greater capacity and potential throughout an organization. He distinguishes *leader development*, which he describes as investment in human capital to enhance intrapersonal competence for selected individuals, from *leadership development*. This, he suggests, is investment in social capital which can develop interpersonal networks and co-operation. Day argues for the necessity of both but suggests that the latter is too often neglected. We would also advocate more emphasis on the development of leadership rather than the individual potential to 'be a leader' as fundamental to furthering the mission of early childhood services. We put forward our paradigm of *leadership within* to help bridge the conceptual gap between leaders and leadership and to offer new ways to think about and debate leadership in practice. The continuing focus on the workforce (DFE 2011; Tickell 2011) provides opportunities to build on the professionalization of early years practitioners (McDowall Clark and Baylis 2010) by integrating leadership with learning as part of professionalism and professional identity (Murray in press). In this way 'the rate of external social and cultural change. . .provides a stimulus for radically rethinking early childhood leadership' (Aubrey 2011: 171).

Leadership within – deriving models for leadership development

A paradigm offers an overall perspective in which to view the subject, therefore *leadership within* provides a conceptual framework from which models of leadership development could be derived. Conceptual frameworks which have the leader as their prime focus will concentrate on the individual learner and on developing leader competencies. The resulting programmes are more likely to use language pertaining to 'acquisition' of skills and 'delivery'. Conceptual frameworks which focus on the process of leadership will produce leadership development models which aim to engage and develop the learning community and utilize the environment in which it operates. Table 10.1 depicts this diagrammatically in order to indicate how fundamental ideas about leadership are further embedded through the training and development model adopted.

If we wish to move towards seeing leadership as social practice to reflect the essential nature of ECEC, then theories which take a societal perspective of learning, such as Engeström's (2000) cycle of expansive learning, may offer useful models for multiprofessional and leadership development. Engeström's (2000) model of 'knotworking' starts from collective questioning of existing practice by a group of people with common purpose. They analyse contradictions in order to develop a means to move forward. A new model for practice arises and is examined and implemented, followed by a period for reflection and consolidation. This is a problem-orientated approach which seeks root causes to common concerns. The contradictions in everyday practice are addressed through collaborative analysis and modelling, creating a shared vision of how to move forward. This approach engages different professional

Table 10.1   A comparison of 'leader' and 'leadership' development programmes

Programme	Leader development	Leadership development
Learning focus	Leader	Leadership
Outcome focus	Product	Process
Learning objectives	Skills Competencies	Cultural Dialogic Relational Situational
Language	Acquisition Mastery Delivery	Engagement Understanding Participation
Teaching approach	Individual Personal	Social practice Individual as a member of community

or community members in the process, enabling multiple voices to be heard. Any collective problem-solving process requires a culture of openness and trust to be developed in which members feel free to participate actively, knowing that they will listen to different perspectives and be listened to; that negotiation and agreement on action will be required, thus creating shared leadership responsibility for implementation. The challenge is how to incorporate the development of agency, relational trust and integrity, which these processes require, as the focus for leadership development rather than the specific tasks and skill set generally viewed to be necessary for the leader/manager. Aubrey (2011: 171) indicates that:

> As more coherent images of practice emerge there will be a requirement for a broader notion of what constitutes effective leadership practice and generation of a more sophisticated set of analytical and conceptual tools to assess its impact.

We put forward the three interweaving features of *leadership within,* namely catalytic agency, reflective integrity and relational interdependence, as possible conceptual tools in moving towards that aim. We believe that they are capable of application in a range of situations in the general training and development of practitioners.

Personal and social knowledge creation and learning involves deconstruction and reconstruction in a continuous process of change and adaptation. It does not exist in isolation from prior knowledge and experience which has in turn been socially and culturally mediated. We therefore need to incorporate the social and situational dimensions of learning into leadership development to acknowledge that learners cannot be separated from the cultural context of work or the social world of leadership which they are trying to know better. This also implies employing learning methods in training courses and in the workplace which draw on dialogue and group activity to find constructive ways of working together and where strategies can be developed, applied and the impact fed back. Knowledge is generated from a dialogue of intelligences, those of the multiple individuals engaged in a common enterprise in an interdependent relationship. Dialogue is therefore a central component of relationship development which supports leadership-rich learning communities to emerge.

Starratt (2007: 182) challenges us to look more closely at what is meant by learning in developing theories of leadership. He sees educational purpose as 'leading a community of learners engaged in a moral and intellectual understanding of who they are and what their relationships and responsibilities [are] to the natural, social and cultural worlds'. It makes sense, therefore, to build leadership development around this purpose and to derive models of training and development which foster understanding of the dynamic of the individual within community.

Applying the paradigm features to leadership development

Leadership development can take place in many places and forms:

- in the workplace through daily interaction;
- in staff development days, coaching, mentoring, supervision;
- through networks and partnerships;
- through joint projects and collaborative working;
- through specifically designed leadership programmes;
- through initial training and ongoing professional development.

We suggest that attention can be paid to the three features of *leadership within* in all these situations.

If we consider the nature of education and care professions and organizations to have an inherently moral purpose (Fullan 1999; Starratt 2007), then leadership development requires us to attend not only to the furtherance of learning but also to the well-being of the community of learners. The pedagogical imperative of passionate care extends beyond furthering the development of children and families to the organizational members and the wider associated community involved in that same purpose. The organizational culture should be modelled and exemplified in dealing with all those who come into contact or are associated with the organization. Models for leadership development therefore need to position the individual in sub-systems and wider social systems to support recognition of their connectivity to others and the relevance of all individual action in relation to the whole. This reinforces the significance of relational interdependence.

Exploration of the formation of professional identity and the ethic of care also has a place in leadership development to examine the basis of professional ideals and mission. Leadership development should therefore place value on the language of caring, examining the power of passionate care in creating emotional drive through catalytic agency to effect change in oneself and influence others. Catalytic agency promotes the common purpose of making a positive difference to children's lives, so developing strategies to promote professional confidence would help to enhance that agency. Learning mechanisms that promote peer or mentor support are useful for providing feedback opportunities which can encourage self-belief and perseverance to overcome obstacles. Methods for practitioner research can also help to provide strategies to put catalytic agency into effect and assess impact. Collaborative projects in particular offer a means to act with others to develop aspects of practice in meaningful and manageable ways, so the impact is tangible.

Situational analysis can be a powerful tool to encourage groups, teams or communities to explore values and practice dilemmas in context, highlighting the interplay of tensions and influences and giving opportunities to practise reflective integrity. When the moral purpose of ECEC is strongly present in a group or community it should reduce unscrupulous use of knowledge for self-serving purposes but focus instead on using it for the good of others. It also provides a motivating effect to recognize dilemmas and work to find strategies to ameliorate them. Reflective integrity can become a developmental process which strengthens social competence in dealing with complex dilemmas and different perspectives, supporting 'authentic relationships' (Starratt 2007) in the workplace. A children's centre leader who acted as a critical reader for aspects of this book recommended the use of reflective integrity in 'supervision' meetings, to enhance cognitive and emotional skill in dealing with and learning from the complexity of professional practice.

There are thus many ways and means of promoting leadership development using the concepts of catalytic agency, reflective integrity and relational interdependence. Leadership development is concerned to increase human and social capital, enabling a participative and sustainable type of leadership to emerge. We suggest, therefore, that leadership development is social and relational and needs to be positioned within teamwork and community.

Conclusion

We are not presenting *leadership within* as a definitive paradigm for early years leadership but offer it as a means to reframe thinking beyond traditional concepts of leadership. As Sergiovanni (2001: 40) suggests, 'it is no easy task to identify a single view of leadership that beats all other views all of the time' and that is not our intention. In developing this paradigm, we seek to give freedom and confidence to practitioners to build leadership ideas and practices from within the profession rather than adopting those from outside; ideas of leadership which are based upon the essential nature and common purpose of ECEC. This releases possibilities for identifying models of leadership development and ways of working which further enhance that purpose. We offer the three key features which characterize *leadership within* as a potential framework for exploring and reworking ideas about leadership in relation to early years practice and to open up scope for potential new models for leadership development.

Glossary

CAF – Common Assessment Framework A framework set up to enable communication and information sharing between professionals as outlined in the 2004 Children Act. CAF is used when children are not making the expected progress and where involvement of multiple agencies is likely to be necessary. CAF is intended to ensure all relevant parties are aware of the 'whole picture' and to prevent children undergoing repetitive and unnecessary assessments. It includes the perspective of parents and child and a lead professional is appointed to act as a single point of contact for the family.

Children's Centres (also Integrated Children's Centres or Family Centres) Children's Centres provide a variety of advice and services to support children and their parents/carers. They aim to bring a holistic approach through different agencies such as health, education and family support. Many provide additional services related to family matters, parenting, training and job opportunities. There are more than 3600 Children's Centres in England including ones which are state-maintained and those with charitable status.

Children's Trusts Local government-level partnerships of different agencies set up by the New Labour government to work together and support frontline practitioners under the leadership of a Children's Services Director. The coalition government has removed the requirement on local authorities to set up Children's Trust Boards as well as the expectation that those Boards should prepare and publish a joint Children and Young People's Plan.

CWDC – Children's Workforce Development Council Set up under the New Labour government to oversee and co-ordinate professional qualifications and development of the wider children's workforce. From April 2012 both the CWDC and the Teaching and Development Agency for Schools (TDA) will be incorporated into a new body to be called the Teaching Agency, bringing together statutory and early years provision.

ECEC – early childhood education and care A term commonly used to refer to provision for children from birth through to the beginnings of statutory schooling. In Britain, the term 'early years' has been commonplace in an attempt to get away from the persistent split between education and care, now officially eliminated through the Childcare Act (2006). The two terms are used interchangeably throughout the book.

ECM – *Every Child Matters* An inclusive strategy developed by the previous government with the intention that all children under the age of 19 should receive the support they need to achieve five outcomes – be healthy; stay safe; enjoy and achieve; make a positive contribution and achieve economic well-being. The *Every Child Matters* green paper underpinned the 2004 Children Act and specified a requirement for multiagency working to support the best outcomes for children. The coalition government has now moved away from this terminology to talk about 'helping children to achieve more' (Puffett 2010).

EPPE – Effective Provision of Pre-school Education project A long-term research project investigating the effectiveness of early education. The EPPE project identified how quality early years settings and graduate level practitioners can support children's social and cognitive development (Sylva *et al.* 2010) and has been very influential in a range of policy initiatives from the EYFS to EYP standards.

EYFS – Early Years Foundation Stage A comprehensive statutory framework for children from birth to 5 (therefore including the first year of statutory schooling). All registered early years settings, maintained and independent schools in England are required to meet the learning, development and welfare requirements in the EYFS. The Tickell Review (Tickell 2011) has recently reported on the EYFS and a revised version will be in use from September 2012. The other nations of the UK have their own variants such as the Foundation Phase in Wales.

EYPS – Early Years Professional Status A specialized graduate status for pedagogues working in early years settings. EYPs are expected to lead and model good practice across their setting.

Integrated Children's Centres see Children's Centres

NPQICL – National Professional Qualification in Integrated Centre Leadership A specialized qualification for those heading up Children's Centres delivering integrated services. NPQICL has equivalency to the National Professional Qualification for Headship for maintained nursery schools.

PVI – private, voluntary and independent sector An acronym used to refer to settings that are not statutory and centrally funded. The PVI sector was initially particularly identified by CWDC for the promotion of

EYPS because of the low proportion of graduates working within these settings.

Reggio Emilia A region in northern Italy where a network of pre-schools, based on strong community principles, developed in the aftermath of the Second World War. Now internationally renowned for high-quality early years practice, the Reggio approach is promoted through travelling exhibitions and planned study tours.

References

Ailwood, J. (2008) Mothers, teachers, maternalism and early childhood education and care: some historical connections, *Contemporary Issues in Early Childhood*, 8(2): 157–65.

Allen, G. (2011) *Early Intervention: The Next Steps*. London: Cabinet Office.

Anning, A., Cottrell, D., Frost, N., Green, J. and Robinson, M. (2006) *Developing Multi-professional Teamwork for Integrated Children's Services*. Maidenhead: Open University Press.

Argyris, C. and Schön, D.A. (1974) *Theory in Practice: Increasing Professional Effectiveness*. San Francisco, CA: Jossey-Bass.

Argyris, C. and Schön, D.A. (1996) *Organizational Learning II: Theory, Method, and Practice*. Reading, MA: Addison-Wesley Publishing Company.

Aubrey, C. (2011) *Leading and Managing in the Early Years*, 2nd edn. London: Sage Publications.

Avery, G. (2004) *Understanding Leadership: Paradigms and Cases*. London: Sage Publications.

Baldock, P. (2011) *Developing Early Childhood Services*. Maidenhead: Open University Press, McGraw-Hill.

Baldock, P., Fitzgerald, D. and Kay, J. (2009) *Understanding Early Years Policy*, 2nd edn. London: Sage Publications.

Ball, C. (1994) *Start Right: The Importance of Early Learning*. London: Royal Society for the Encouragement of the Arts.

Ball, S.J. and Vincent, C. (2005) The 'childcare champion'? New Labour, social justice and the childcare market, *British Educational Research Journal*, 31(5): 557–70.

Bennett, N., Wise, C., Woods, P. and Harvey, J. (2003) *Distributed Leadership*. Nottingham: National College for School Leadership.

Bennis, W. (2007) The challenges of leadership in the modern world, *American Psychologist*, 62(1): 2–5.

BERA (British Educational Research Association) (2004) *Revised Ethical Guidelines for Educational Research*. Nottingham: British Educational Research Association.

Berger, P. and Luckman, T. (1966) *The Social Construction of Reality: A Treatise in the Sociology of Knowledge*. London: Allen Lane.

Billett, S. (2006) Relational interdependence between social and individual agency in work and working life, *Mind, Culture and Activity*, 13(1): 53–69.

Billett, S. (2008) Learning throughout working life: a relational interdependence between personal and social agency, *British Journal of Educational Studies*, 56(1): 39–58.

Broadhead, P. (2009) Conflict resolution and children's behaviour: observing and understanding social and co-operative play in early years educational settings, *Early Years*, 29(2): 105–18.

Bronfenbrenner, U. (1979) *The Ecology of Human Development*. Cambridge, MA: Harvard University Press.

Brown, L.M. and Posner, B.Z. (2001) Exploring the relationship between learning and leadership, *Leadership and Organisation Development Journal*, 22(6): 274–80.

Bruce, T. (2005) *Early Childhood Education*, 3rd edn. London: Hodder Arnold.

Burman, E. (2001) Beyond the baby and the bathwater: postdualistic developmental psychologies for diverse childhoods, *European Early Childhood Education Research Journal*, 9(1): 5–22.

Bush, T. (2003) *Theories of Educational Leadership and Management*. London: Sage Publications.

CACE (Central Advisory Council for Education) (1967) *Children and their Primary Schools* (Plowden Report). London: HMSO.

Cameron, C. (2001) Promise or problem? A review of the literature on men working in early childhood services, *Gender, Work and Organization*, 8(4): 430–53.

Cameron, C. (2004) *Building an Integrated Workforce for a Long-term Vision of Universal Early Education and Care*. London: Day Care Trust.

Cameron, C. (2006) Men in the nursery revisited: issues of male workers and professionalism, *Contemporary Issues in Early Childhood*, 7(1): 68–79.

Cameron, C., Moss, P. and Owen, C. (1999) *Men in the Nursery: Gender and Caring Work*. London: Paul Chapman.

Cameron, D. (2008) *The Myth of Mars and Venus: Do Men and Women Really Speak Different Languages?* Oxford: Oxford University Press.

Canning, N. (2009) Empowering communities through inspirational leadership, in A. Robins and S. Callan (eds) *Managing Early Years Settings*. London: Sage Publications.

CCEA (Council for the Curriculum, Examinations and Assessment) (2006) *The Revised NI Primary Curriculum*. Belfast: Department of Education, Northern Ireland.

Clarke, B., Chambers, P., Consoli, F., Tommasini, M. and Scarcina, R. (2007) A rationale for reflective practice in vocational education and training, in H. Stroobants, P. Chambers and B. Clarke (eds) *Reflective Journeys*. Rome: Leonardo da Vinci Reflect Project.

Colley, H. (2006) Learning to labour with feeling: class, gender and emotion in childcare education and training, *Contemporary Issues in Early Childhood*, 7(1): 15–29.

Connell, R. (2009) *Gender*, 2nd edn. Cambridge: Polity Press.

Covey, S.R. (1992) *Principle-centred leadership*. London: Simon & Schuster.

Creswell, J.W. (2009) *Research Design*. London: Sage Publications.

Cross, S.E., Gore, J.S. and Morris, M.L. (2003) The relational-interdependent self-construal, self-concept consistency and well-being, *Journal of Personality and Social Psychology*, 85(5): 933–44.

Cubillo, L. (1999) Gender and leadership in the NPQH: an opportunity lost?, *Journal of In-service Education*, 25(3): 381–91.

CWDC (Children's Workforce Development Council) (2010) *On the Right Track – Guidance to the Standards for the Award of Early Years Professional Status*. Leeds: CWDC.

Dahlberg, G. and Moss, P. (2005) *Ethics and Politics in Early Childhood Education*. London: Routledge.

Day, C. (2004) The passion of successful leadership, *School Leadership and Management*, 24(4): 427–37.

Day, C., Harris, A., Hadfield, M., Tolley, H. and Beresford, J. (2000) *Leading Schools in Times of Change*. Buckingham: Open University Press.

Day, D. (2001) Leadership development: a review in context, *Leadership Quarterly*, 11(4): 581–613.

DCSF (Department for Children, Schools and Families) (2007) *The Children's Plan: Building Better Futures*. London: DCSF.

DES (Department of Education and Science) (1990) *Starting with Quality: Report of the Committee of Enquiry into the Quality of Educational Experience Offered to Three and Four year Olds* (Rumbold Report). London: DES/HMSO.

Dewey, J. (1933) *How we Think*. Boston, MA: Heath and Co.

DFE (Department for Education) (2011) *Supporting Families in the Foundation Years*. http://www.education.gov.uk/childrenandyoungpeople/earlylearning-andchildcare/early/a00192398/supporting-families-in-the-foundation-years

DfEE (Department for Education and Employment) (1998) *Meeting the Childcare Challenge*. London: The Stationery Office.

DfES (Department for Education and Skills) (2003) *Every Child Matters (green paper)*. London: HMSO.

DfES (2004) *The Children Act*. London: HMSO.

DfES (2006) *The Childcare Act 2006*. London: DfES.

DfES (2008) *The Early Years Foundation Stage*. Nottingham: DCSF Publications.

DoH (Department of Health) (1989) *The Children Act*. London: HMSO.

Dunlop, A-W. (2005) *Scottish Early Childhood Teachers' Concepts of Leadership: Interim Report of Research in Progress*. Glasgow: University of Strathclyde.

Dunlop, A-W. (2008) *A Literature Review on Leadership in the Early Years*. Dundee: Learning and Teaching Scotland.

Dweck, C.S. (2002) *Self Theories: Their Role in Motivation, Personality and Development*. New York: Psychology Press.

Dweck, C.S. (2008) Can personality be changed?, *Association for Psychological Science*, 17(6): 391–4.

Eacott, S. (2010) Bourdieu's strategies and the challenge for educational leadership, *International Journal of Leadership in Education*, 13(3): 265–81.

Eagleton, T. (1990) *The Significance of Theory*. Oxford: Blackwell.

Ebbeck, M. and Waniganayake, M. (2003) *Early Childhood Professionals: Leading Today and Tomorrow*. Sydney: MacLennan and Petty.

Edgar, A. and Pattison, S. (2011) Integrity and the moral complexity of professional practice, *Nursing Philosophy*, 12(2): 94–106.

Edwards, A. and D'Arcy, C. (2004) Relational agency and disposition in socio-cultural accounts of learning to teach, *Educational Review*, 56(2): 147–55.

Edwards, C., Gandini, L. and Forman, G. (eds) (1993) *The Hundred Languages of Children*. Norwood, NJ: Ablex .

Elfer, P., Goldschmied, E. and Selleck, D. (2003) *Key Persons in the Nursery: Building Relationships for Quality Provision*. London: David Fulton.

Engeström, Y. (2000) Activity theory as a framework for analyzing and redesigning work, *Ergonomics*, 43(7): 960–74.

Field, F. (2010) *The Foundation Years: Preventing Poor Children Becoming Poor Adults*. The report of the independent review on poverty and life chances. London: Cabinet Office. Available at http://www.frankfield.co.uk/review-on-poverty-and-life-chances/ [accessed 20 December 2011].

Freire, P. (1999) *The Pedagogy of the Heart*. New York: Continuum Publishing.

Fromberg, D. (1997) The professional status of early childhood educators, in J. Isenberg and M.R.C. Jalongo (eds) *The Professional and Social Status of the Early Childhood Educator: Challenges, Controversies and Insights*. New York: Columbia Teachers College Press.

Fullan, M. (1999) *Change Forces: The Sequel*. London: Falmer Press.

Gallwey, T. (2002) *The Inner Game of Work*. New York: Texere Publishing.

Gill, R. (2006) *Theory and Practice of Leadership*. London: Sage Publications.

Gilligan, C. (1989) *Mapping the Moral Domain: A Contribution of Women's Thinking to Psychological Theory of Education*. Cambridge, MA: Harvard University Press.

Goldschmied, E. and Jackson, S. (2004) *People Under Three: Young Children in Day Care*, 2nd edn. London: Routledge.

Goleman, D. (1996) *Emotional Intelligence: Why It Can Matter More than IQ*. London: Bloomsbury.

Goleman, D., Boyatzis, R. and McKee, A. (2002) *Primal Leadership: Realizing the Power of Emotional Intelligence*. Boston, MA: Harvard Business School Press.

Gronn, P. (2002) Distributed leadership as a unit of analysis, *The Leadership Quarterly*, 13(4): pp 423–51.

Hager, P. (2004) Conceptions of learning and understanding learning at work, *Studies in Continuing Education*, 26(1): 3–17.

Hall, V. (1996) *Dancing on the Ceiling: A Study of Women Managers in Education*. London: Paul Chapman.

Handy, C. (1993) *Understanding Organisations*, 4th edn. London: Penguin.

Hargreaves, A. and Fink, D. (2006) *Sustainable Leadership*. San Francisco, CA: Jossey-Bass.

Hargreaves, L. and Hopper, B. (2006) Early years, low status? Early years teachers' perceptions of their occupational status, *Early Years*, 26(2): 171–86.

Harris, A. (2008) *Distributed School Leadership*. London: Routledge.

Harris, A. and Bennett, N. (eds) (2001) *School Effectiveness and School Improvement*. New York: Continuum Publishing.

Harris, A., Day, C., Hopkins, D., Hadfield, M., Hargreaves, A. and Chapman, C. (2003) *Effective Leadership for School Improvement*. London: Routledge Falmer.

Harris, B. (2004) Leading by heart, *School Leadership and Management*, 24(4): 391–404.

Henderson-Kelly, L. and Pamphilon, B. (2000) Women's model of leadership in the child care sector, *Australian Journal of Early Childhood*, 25(1): 8–12.

HM Government (2009) *Next Steps for Early Learning and Childcare: Building on the 10-year Strategy*. Nottingham: Department for Children, Schools and Families.

HMT (HM Treasury) (2004) *Choice for Parents, the Best start for Children: a Ten-year Strategy for Children*. London: HMSO.

Hochschild, A.R. (1983) *The Managed Heart: Commercialization of Human Feeling*. Berkeley, CA: University of California Press.

Hujala, E. (2002) Leadership in a child care context in Finland, in V. Nivala and E. Hujala (eds) *Leadership in Early Childhood Education: Cross-Cultural Perspectives*. Oulu, Finland: Oulu University Press.

Hujala, E. and Puroila, A-M. (eds) (1998) *Towards Understanding Leadership in Early Childhood Context: Cross-cultural Perspectives*. Oulu, Finland: Oulu University Press.

Jones, C. and Pound, L. (2008) *Leadership and Management in the Early Years*. Maidenhead: Open University Press.

Jordi, R. (2011) Reframing the concept of reflection: consciousness, experiential learning and reflective learning practices, *Adult Education Quarterly*, 61(2): 181–97.

Kagan, S.L. and Bowman, B.T. (eds) (1997) *Leadership in Early Care and Education*. Washington, DC: National Association for the Education of Young Children.

Kagan, S.L. and Hallmark, L.G. (2001) Cultivating leadership in early care and education, *Child Care Information Exchange*, 140: 7–10.

Kaser, L. and Halbert, J. (2009) *Leadership Mindsets: Innovation and Learning in the Transformation of Schools*. Abingdon: Routledge.

Kelley, R.E. (1992) *The Power of Followership: How to Create Leaders People Want to Follow and Followers Who Lead Themselves*. New York: Currency Doubleday.

Kinsella, E.A. (2010) The art of reflective practice in health and social care: reflections on the legacy of Donald Schön, *Reflective Practice*, 11(4): 565–75.

Lambert, L. (2002) Beyond instructional leadership, *Educational Leadership,* 59(8): 37–40.

Lambert, L. (2003) Leadership redefined: an evocative context for teacher leadership, *School Leadership and Management,* 23(4): 421–30.

Laming, Lord (2003) *The Victoria Climbié Inquiry Report.* London: The Stationery Office.

Lave, J. and Wenger, E. (1991) *Situated Learning: Legitimate Peripheral Participation.* Cambridge: Cambridge University Press.

Lave, J. and Wenger, E. (1996) Practice, person, social world, in H. Daniels (ed.) *Vygotsky.* London: Routledge.

Law, S. and Glover, D. (2000) *Educational Leadership and Learning: Practice, Policy and Research.* Buckingham: Open University Press.

Lillejord, S. and Dysthe, O. (2008) Productive learning practice – a theoretical discussion based on two cases, *Journal of Education and Work,* 21(1): 75–89.

McDowall Clark, R. (2010) *Childhood in Society for Early Childhood Studies.* Exeter: Learning Matters.

McDowall Clark, R. (2011) Working in the spaces; shared values and localized practice. Keynote speech presented to the 11th Conference of the European Affective Education Network, Ljubljana, Slovenia, 26–29 June.

McDowall Clark, R. (in press) 'I'd never thought of myself as a leader . . .': reconceptualizing leadership with early years professionals, *European Early Childhood Education Research Journal.*

McDowall Clark, R. and Baylis, S. (2010) The new professionals: leading for change, in M. Reed and N. Canning (eds) *Reflective Practice in the Early Years.* London: Sage Publications.

McDowall Clark, R. and Baylis, S. (2011) 'Go softly . . .': the reality of 'leading practice' in early years settings, in M. Reed and N. Canning (eds) *Quality Improvement and Change in the Early Years.* London: Sage Publications.

Malaguzzi, L. (1996) *The Hundred Languages of Children.* Reggio Emilia: Reggio Children.

Marquardt, M.J. (2000) Action learning and leadership, *The Learning Organisation,* 7(5): 233–41.

Mathers, S., Ranns, H., Karemaker, A., Moody, A., Sylva, K., Graham, J. and Siraj-Blatchford, I. (2011) *Evaluation of the Graduate Leader Fund. Final Report.* London: Department for Education. Available from https://www.education. gov.uk/publications/standard/publicationDetail/Page1/DFE-RR144 [accessed 20 December 2011].

Mathers, S., Sylva, K. and Joshi, H. (2007) *Quality of Childcare Settings in the Millennium Cohort Study.* DCSF SSU2007/FR/025. Nottingham: DCSF Publications.

Miller, L. and Cable, C. (eds) (2008) *Professionalism in the Early Years.* London: Hodder.

Moss, P. (2001) The otherness of Reggio, in L. Abbott and C. Nutbrown (eds) *Experiencing Reggio Emilia.* Buckingham: Open University Press.

Moss, P. (2006) Structures, understandings and discourse: possibilities for re-envisioning the early childhood worker, *Contemporary Issues in Early Childhood*, 7(1): 30–41.

Moss, P. (2010) We cannot continue as we are: the educator in an education for survival, *Contemporary Issues in Early Childhood*, 11(1): 8–19.

Moyles, J. (2001) Passion, paradox and professionalism in early years education, *Early Years*, 21(2): 81–95.

Moyles, J. (2004) *Effective Leadership and Management in the Early Years*. Maidenhead: Open University Press.

Moyles, J., Adams, S. and Musgrove, A. (2002) *SPEEL: Study of Pedagogical Effectiveness*, Research Report 363. London: Department for Education and Skills.

Muijs, D., Aubrey, C., Harris, A. and Briggs, M. (2004) How do they manage? A review of the research on leadership in early childhood, *Journal of Early Childhood Research* 2(2): 157–69.

Murray, J. (2009) Value-based leadership and management, in A. Robins and S. Callan (eds) *Managing Early Years Settings*. London: Sage Publications.

Murray, J. (in press) Becoming an Early Years Professional: developing a new professional identity, *European Early Childhood Education Research Journal*.

NCSL (National College for School Leadership) (2007) *What We Know About School Leadership*. Nottingham: NCSL. Available at http://www.nationalcollege.org.uk/docinfo?id=17480&filename=what-we-know-about-school-leadership.pdf [accessed 20 December 2011].

Nivala, V. (2002) Leadership in theory, leadership in general, in V. Nivala and E. Hujala (eds) *Leadership in Early Childhood Education: Cross-Cultural Perspectives*. Oulu, Finland: Oulu University Press.

Nivala, V. and Hujala, E. (2002) (eds) *Leadership in Early Childhood Education: Cross-cultural Perspectives*. Oulu, Finland: Department of Educational Sciences and Teacher Education, University of Oulu.

Nupponen, H. (2006) Framework for developing leadership skills in childcare centres in Queensland, Australia, *Contemporary Issues in Early Childhood*, 7(2): 146–61.

Oberheumer, P. (2000) Conceptualizing the professional role in early childhood centres: emerging profiles in four European countries, *Early Childhood Research and Practice*, 2(2): 1–3.

Oberheumer, P. (2005) Conceptualising the early childhood pedagogue: policy approaches and issues of professionalism, *European Early Childhood Education Research Journal*, 13(1): 5–16.

OECD (Organization for Economic Co-operation and Development) (2004) *Starting Strong II: Early Childhood Education and Care*. Paris: OECD.

Open EYE Campaign (2011) The Tickell Review of the Early Years Foundation Stage: an 'Open EYE' dialogue, in R. House (ed.) *Too Much, Too Soon? Early Learning and the Erosion of Childhood*. Stroud: Hawthorn Press.

Osgood, J. (2004) Time to get down to business? The responses of early years practitioners to entrepreneurial approaches to professionalism, *Journal of Early Childhood Research*, 2(1): 5–24.

Osgood, J. (2006a) Deconstructing professionalism in early childhood education: resisting the regulatory gaze, *Contemporary Issues in Early Childhood*, 7(1): 5–14.

Osgood, J. (2006b) Professionalism and performativity: the feminist challenge facing early years practitioners, *Early Years*, 26(2): 187–99.

Osgood, J. (2010) Reconstructing professionalism in ECEC: the case for the 'critically reflective emotional professional', *Early Years*, 30(2): 119–33.

Owen, C. (2003) *Men's Work? Changing the Gender Mix of the Childcare and Early Years Workforce*. Facing the Future: Policy Papers 6. London: Day Care Trust.

Owen, C., Cameron, C. and Moss, P. (eds) (1998) *Men as Workers in Services for Young Children: Issues of a Mixed Gender Workforce*. Bedford Way Papers. London: Institute of Education, University of London.

Parsons, T. and Bales, R.F. (1956) *Family Socialisation and Interaction*. London: Routledge.

Payne, M. (2000) *Teamwork in Multiprofessional Care*. Basingstoke: Palgrave.

Penn, H. (2007) Childcare market management: how the United Kingdom government has reshaped its role in developing early childhood education and care, *Contemporary Issues in the Early Years*, 8(3): 192–207.

Puffet, N. (2010) Government clarifies ban on Every Child Matters, *Children and Young People Now*, 10–23 August.

Pugh, G. (2010) Improving outcomes for young children: can we narrow the gap?, *Early Years*, 30(1): 5–14.

Pugh, G. and Duffy, B. (2010) *Contemporary Issues in the Early Years*. London: Sage Publications.

Raelin, J. (2003) *Creating Leaderful Organizations: How to Bring Out the Leadership in Everyone*: San Francisco, CA: Berrett Koehler.

Reay, D. and Ball, S. (2000) Essentials of female management: women's ways of working in the educational market place, *Educational Management and Administration*, 28(2): 145–59.

Rinaldi, C. (2006) *In Dialogue with Reggio Emilia*. Abingdon: Routledge.

Rodd, J. (2006) *Leadership in Early Childhood*, 3rd edn. Maidenhead: Open University Press.

Rogers, C. (1961) *On Becoming a Person*. Boston, MA: Houghton Mifflin.

Rogers, M.F. (1983) *Sociology, Ethnomethodology and Experience*. Cambridge: Cambridge University Press.

Rolfe, H. (2005) *Men in Childcare*. Working Paper no 35. London: Equal Opportunities Commission.

Rosemary, C.A. and Puroila, A-M. (2002) Leadership potential in day care settings: using dual analysis to explore directors' work in Finland and the USA, in V. Nivala and E. Hujala (eds) *Leadership in Early Childhood Education: Cross-cultural Perspectives*. Oulu, Finland: Oulu University Press.

Rosenberg, L.R. (2010) Transforming leadership: reflective practice and the enhancement of happiness, *Reflective Practice*, 11(1): 9–18.

Sargent, P. (2005) The gendering of men in early childhood education, *Sex Roles*, 52(3–4): 251–9.

Schön, D.A. (1991) *The Reflective Practitioner: How Professionals Think in Action*. Aldershot: Avebury.

Scottish Executive (2005) *A Curriculum for Excellence*. Edinburgh: Scottish Executive.

Scrivens, C. (2002) Constructions of leadership: does gender make a difference? Perspectives from an English-speaking country, in V. Nivala and E. Hujala (eds) *Leadership in Early Childhood Education: Cross-Cultural Perspectives*. Oulu, Finland: Oulu University Press.

Senge, P.M. (1993) *The Fifth Discipline: The Art and Practice of the Learning Organization*. London: Century Business.

Sergiovanni, T.J. (1998) Leadership as pedagogy, capital development and school effectiveness, *International Journal of Leadership in Education*, 1(1): 37–46.

Sergiovanni, T.J. (2001) *Leadership. What's In It for Schools?* Abingdon: Routledge Falmer.

Shakeshaft, C. (1989) *Women in Educational Administration*. Beverly Hills, CA: Sage Publications.

Simpson, D. (2010) Being professional? Conceptualising early years professionalism in England, *European Early Childhood Education Research Journal*, 18(1): 5–14.

Siraj-Blatchford, I. and Manni, L. (2007) *Effective Leadership in the Early Years Sector (ELEYS) Study: Research Report*. London: Institute of Education, University of London/General Teaching Council for England.

Siraj-Blatchford, I., Sylva, K., Muttock, S., Gilden, R. and Bell, D. (2002) *Researching Effective Pedagogy in the Early Years (REPEY)*. DfES Research Report 356. London: DfES/HMSO.

Slater, L. (2008) Pathways to building leadership capacity, *Education Management Administration and Leadership*, 36(1): 55–69.

Spelman, E. (1988) *Inessential Woman: Problems of Exclusion in Feminist Thought*. London: Women's Press.

Spillane, J.P. (2006) *Distributed Leadership*. San Francisco, CA: Jossey-Bass.

Spillane, J.P., Halverson, R. and Diamond, J.B. (2001) Investigating school leadership practice: a distributed perspective, *Educational Researcher*, 30(3): 23–8.

Spillane, J.P., Halverson, R. and Diamond, J.B. (2004) Towards a theory of leadership practice: a distributed perspective, *Journal of Curriculum Studies*, 36(1): 3–34.

Springate, I., Atkinson, M., Straw, S., Lamont, E. and Grayson, H. (2008) *Narrowing the Gap in Outcomes: Early Years, 0–5 years*. Slough: NFER.

Starratt, R.J. (2007) Leading a community of learners, *Educational Management Administration and Leadership*, 35(2): 165–183.

Strauss, A. and Corbin, J. (1990) *Basics of Qualitative Research: Grounded Theory, Procedures and Techniques*. London: Sage Publications.

Sumsion, J. (2000) Negotiating otherness: a male early childhood worker's gender positioning, *International Journal of Early Years Education*, 8(2): 129–40.

Sylva, K. and Pugh, G. (2005) Transforming the early years in England, *Oxford Review of Education*, 31(1): 11–27.

Sylva, K., Melhuish, E.C., Sammons, P., Siraj-Blatchford, I. and Taggart, B. (2004) *The Effective Provision of Pre-school Education (EPPE) Project: Final Report*. London: DfES and Institute of Education, University of London.

Sylva, K., Melhuish, E.C., Sammons, P., Siraj-Blatchford I., and Taggart, B. (2010) *Early Childhood Matters: Evidence from the Effective Pre-school and Primary Education Project*. London: Routledge.

Taggart, G. (2011) Don't we care? The ethics and emotional labour of early years professionalism, *Early Years*, 31(1): 85–95.

Teather, S. (2011) Written ministerial statement, 18 July. Available at http://publications.parliament.uk/ [accessed 20 December 2011].

Tickell, C. (2011) *The Early Years: Foundations for Life, Health and Learning. An Independent Review on the Early Years Foundation Stage to Her Majesty's Government*. Available from http://www.education.gov.uk/tickellreview [accessed 20 December 2011].

Urban, M. (2008) Dealing with uncertainty: challenges and possibilities for the early childhood profession, *European Early Childhood Education Research Journal*, 16(2): 135–52.

Vygotsky, L.S. (1978) *Mind in Society: The Development of Higher Psychological Processes*. Cambridge, MA: Harvard University Press.

WAG (Welsh Assembly Government) (2008) *Framework for Children's Learning for 3- to 7-year olds in Wales*. Cardiff: WAG.

Wajcman, J. (1999) *Managing Like a Man: Women and Men in Corporate Management*. Cambridge: Polity Press.

Walsh, G. (2007) Northern Ireland, in M.M. Clark and T. Waller (eds) *Early Education and Care: Policy and Practice*. London: Sage Publications.

Waniganayake, M. (2002) Growth of leadership: with training, can anyone become a leader?, in V. Nivala and E. Hujala (eds) *Leadership in Early Childhood Education: Cross-cultural Perspectives*. Oulu, Finland: Oulu University Press.

Wenger, E. (1998) *Communities of Practice: Learning, Meaning and Identity*. Cambridge: Cambridge University Press.

Western, S. (2008) *Leadership – a Critical Text*. London: Sage Publications.

Whalley, M. (1999) Women leaders in early childhood settings: a dialogue in the 1990s. Unpublished PhD thesis, University of Wolverhampton.

Whalley, M. (2007) *Involving Parents in their Children's Learning*, 2nd edn. London: Sage Publications.

Whalley, M.E. (2008) *Leading Practice in Early Years Settings*. Exeter: Learning Matters.

Whelan, C. (2006) *Pedagogical Leadership*. Nottingham: National College for School Leadership.

Willis, H. (2009) Who cares who pays? Paper presented to the Daycare Trust National Conference, 17 November.

Yelland, N. (ed.) (1998) *Gender in Early Childhood*. London: Routledge Falmer.

Index